Never Bet the Farm

How Entrepreneurs Take Risks, Make Decisions—and How You Can, Too

Anthony L. Iaquinto

Stephen Spinelli Jr.

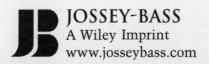

JOSSEY-BASS
A Wiley Imprint
www.josseybass.com

Published by Jossey-Bass
A Wiley Imprint
989 Market Street, San Francisco, CA 94103-1741   www.josseybass.com

Jossey-Bass books and products are available through most bookstores. To contact Jossey-Bass directly call our Customer Care Department within the U.S. at 800-956-7739, outside the U.S. at 317-572-3986, or fax 317-572-4002.

Jossey-Bass also publishes its books in a variety of electronic formats. Some content that appears in print may not be available in electronic books.

Library of Congress Cataloging-in-Publication Data

Iaquinto, Anthony L., 1955-
    Never bet the farm : how entrepreneurs take risks, make decisions—and how you can, too / Anthony L. Iaquinto, Stephen Spinelli Jr.
        p. cm.
    Includes bibliographical references and index.
    ISBN-13: 978-0-7879-8366-6 (pbk.)
    ISBN-10: 0-7879-8366-7 (pbk.)
    1. New business enterprises.   2. Entrepreneurship.   3. Small business—Management.
4. Business planning.   I. Spinelli, Stephen.   II. Title.
    HD62.5.I27 2006
    658.4'21—dc22   2006000728

Printed in the United States of America
FIRST EDITION
PB Printing   10 9 8 7 6 5 4 3 2 1

Contents

Introduction by
Anthony L. Iaquinto

We're living in a world with unimaginable adversity and invisible threats requiring disaster preparation: cities post evacuation routes, hospitals stockpile vaccines, and companies maintain backup data centers. We prepare for the worst so we can limit any damage and preserve the will and the resources for a quick and full recovery. By readying ourselves for a catastrophe, we might even avert the nightmare itself.

Unfortunately, anyone who suggests that entrepreneurs should prepare for adversity gets slammed as being defeatist by positive thinkers. But why should entrepreneurs be any different from a sailor who stows a well-stocked emergency pack or a mill worker who puts a little bit aside each month for a rainy day or a Boy Scout following his motto, "Be prepared"? Making advance provision for trouble makes sense; in fact, not doing so is foolhardy.

Never Bet the Farm is designed to help you prepare for setbacks by providing you with a framework that can help you reduce risks and simplify decision making. This easily understandable book begins with an acknowledgment that the vast majority of new businesses will not meet their founders' expectations, even when the financing becomes deeper, the attitudes more positive, and the planning more sophisticated, and that experiencing a bankruptcy does not mean you have failed; winners are those who can keep themselves in the game for another shot at success. Entrepreneurs should prepare for misfortune because that preparation could limit the costs of—and probably prevent—the very thing we fear most: business failure.

How Does *Never Bet the Farm* Compare to Other Books?

Most available books on entrepreneurship fall into two general categories: textbooks and inspirational books.

Textbooks (for example, the best-selling *New Venture Creation for the 21st Century* by Spinelli and Timmons, 2003) and other how-to publications generally do a great job of explaining the basics of starting a business, including how to find opportunities, analyze the environment, write a business plan, or invest in a franchise. But these books can sometimes be dry and hard to slog through. In addition, textbooks are designed as tools to be used in a classroom, with a professor as the interface between the written word and the reader. Our book is different. We want to inform the reader directly. Finally, although textbooks can tell you *how* to do something, they aren't very good about telling you *what* to do. That's a bit like going to your favorite uncle for advice, and all he can say is, "It depends."

In hundreds of interviews, I have found that if individuals do not have an overarching perspective on entrepreneurship to guide their decision making, they often have a difficult time deciding which option they should follow. In turn, this leads to confusion, frustration, or both, thus preventing many potential entrepreneurs from moving forward. In the United States, while almost thirty million people are actively working on starting a business, only about three million businesses actually get launched from this effort (see the Global Entrepreneurship Monitor [GEM Report], 2004). In *Never Bet the Farm*, we present a logical and easy-to-understand framework that aspiring entrepreneurs can use as a basis for their decision making.

As for the inspirational variety, these books frequently claim to have "the five secrets" to a successful start-up, but the five secrets in one book don't often jibe with the five secrets of the others, leaving us with the impression that either none of the authors know their subject or that there are literally hundreds of secrets to success.

Finally, several books deal with failure in business, though not in the same way as *Never Bet the Farm*. Some, like *Entrepreneurs in History: Success vs. Failures* (Klees, 1995) are case studies. Others, such as *Fail-Proof Your Business* (Adams, 1999), focus on how to prevent or avoid bankruptcy. *Learning from Failure* (Hatamura, 2002) and others of its type are guides to coping after suffering a setback. Although excellent for those who have already closed a business, these books have a reactionary perspective.

Never Bet the Farm takes a proactive approach to business failure, contending that if entrepreneurs begin by preparing for setbacks, using a framework that can reduce risks and simplify decision making, they can increase the probability of achieving success.

Who Should Read This Book?

Never Bet the Farm is an easy-to-understand and attractive tool for anyone who has business ideas: office workers, homemakers, mechanics, engineers, bartenders, and business school students. It's designed for entrepreneurs who understand that despite all the skills, resources, planning, and positive thinking they can muster, success may not come the first time around. Most important, it's intended for people who invent, integrate, craft, sew, design, process, cook, or make things that their family and friends snap up faster than they can produce but who might be wary of the risks involved in starting their own business or overwhelmed by the multitude of decisions they face.

The framework presented in *Never Bet the Farm* is made up of fifteen principles, organized into two parts: "Developing the Correct Frame of Mind" and "Making the Right Decisions." Some of these tenets have been around since the buggy whip was usurped by the accelerator; others are a reaction to the dot.com boom-and-bust of the 1990s; still others have sprung from our own research and experiences. There are no guarantees, but by following the framework discussed in this book, you can significantly increase the chances of becoming a successful entrepreneur.

Who Am I?

I started my first business venture when I was just sixteen, selling candy, popcorn, and sodas out of a wooden shed behind the backstop at a softball field in a Minneapolis suburb. I didn't make much money, but the experience provided me with a great introduction to entrepreneurship. In lieu of a more typical college summer job, my second venture involved selling customized T-shirts to outfitters and resorts in northern Minnesota. I took orders from my customers, purchased T-shirts wholesale, and silk-screened them. This venture was considerably more profitable than the first and provided funds to see me through my last two years as an undergraduate and several more years of graduate studies.

After completing my Ph.D. at Columbia University, I moved to Japan, where I taught at a local university and opened three businesses: an adult education center and two restaurants. Two were successful; the other was not.

I have spent my adult life fluctuating between being a cloistered scholar and an energetic entrepreneur. At first glance, my dual pursuits may appear to signal an acute case of multiple personality disorder, but these two careers have not been mutually exclusive. The more I study entrepreneurship, the more understanding I gain about what should happen when you start your own business. The more turns I took as an entrepreneur, the wiser I got about what really occurs. Sometimes these two paths compliment each other, and at other times they contradict each other. But it is in paradoxes that I have discovered some of the fifteen principles we present in our book.

Introduction by
Stephen Spinelli Jr.

I accepted Anthony's offer to join him in writing this book because *Never Bet the Farm* is, above all else, a celebration of entrepreneurship as a professional endeavor. Too often, entrepreneurs are portrayed as reckless cowboys, born champions, or worst of all, rock stars.

Although luck plays a role in most lives and professions, a vast majority of entrepreneurs toil diligently to create value. They become learning machines because they understand that knowledge is the underpinning of sound decision making, even in the most wildly ambiguous environments. It is easy to be lured by entrepreneurship's driving principle of value creation, including the possibility of personal wealth. But experienced creators of wealth are never attracted to a deal without understanding the risk involved. Indeed, finding the "unfair advantage" inspires most start-ups. An unfair advantage tilts the start-up toward the high-potential venture and exceptional returns.

Craig Benson—cofounder of Cabletron, former governor of New Hampshire, and friend of mine—explains risk and reward in a personal story.

Craig was afraid of heights. He knew this fear was irrational and impeded his enjoyment of life. So he took action. With his college roommate, he decided to learn how to hang glide. As he explains it, hang gliding is falling at a slower rate than the angle of the approaching ground below. When properly executed, it results in a smooth flight, followed by a short run.

Craig took lessons, practiced often, and eventually became quite adept at hang gliding. His fear of heights was ameliorated by the joy and freedom of the flight.

But the ultimate test of a hang glider is to take off and fly from a cliff—no gently sloping, pastoral setting but a jagged, mountainous precipice. The reward is an extended and intensified experience, as well as fulfillment in conquering the ultimate challenge in this sport.

Craig hired one of the world's finest hang-gliding experts to guide him. He bought the best protective gear and clothing. He intensified his training.

When he arrived at the sheer cliff, his instructor reminded him that he must jump from the cliff *and point himself straight down*. If you try to glide directly across from the launch, you will fall slightly, then be flipped backwards, crashing, maybe fatally, into the side of the mountain.

Well trained as he was, Craig hurled himself over the edge, pointed straight down, and was lifted into perfect flight. He soared beyond the face of the cliff and experienced near-overwhelming exhilaration.

When he had landed safely, he watched other gliders. He noticed a man with shorts and a T-shirt, no shoes, and no helmet take off. The glider performed exquisitely. He sliced through the air, turned, and headed back toward the cliff. He glided across the side of the mountain, cutting along the ragged stone face. Several minutes later the scantily clad expert glider landed gracefully.

"Why?" asked Craig. "Why tempt fate by eschewing safety gear and gliding so close to the mountainside?" A month later Craig read that the expert glider had died in a gliding accident. He had needlessly bet the farm—and lost. He was tragically out of the game.

Craig Benson's story is an intense depiction of entrepreneurship's "thought-and-action" paradigm. For an entrepreneur, thought without action is frivolous; action without thought is dangerous.

Never Bet the Farm also illustrates the importance of wisdom in entrepreneurship (often confused with luck or instinct). Indeed, I believe this book will add to your personal intellectual capital by helping you learn from the experiences of others. Remember, wisdom is the collection and application of knowledge in a specific context. Thomas Edison tried over two thousand experiments to create a filament for the electric light. He never considered these experiments as failures; rather, they enhanced his understanding of what would help him eventually become successful.

My role in this book is to probe and challenge Anthony's experiences and perspectives. I have attempted to act as an honest broker of ideas and, occasionally, a conscience. Ultimately, I conclude that Anthony understands the role of risk, which is to motivate the complex expertise of the entrepreneur into thoughtful action. It's a pleasure to be part of this book.

Part One

DEVELOPING THE CORRECT FRAME OF MIND

Nothing that sends you to the grave with a smile on
your face comes easy. Work hard doing what you
love. Find out what gives you energy and improve
on it.

Betty Coster, Entrepreneur

To be a successful entrepreneur requires the correct frame of mind, which involves confidence in one's ideas, the courage to take the plunge, and the willingness to work hard. It also includes several notions not usually touted by other coaches, such as these: *Entrepreneurship is a career* and *Luck is part of the equation*. Developing the correct attitude prepares businesspeople mentally and emotionally for the trials of starting their own business. The ideas presented in this section also enable them to understand the wisdom of making the *right* decisions.

Developing the proper frame of mind for entrepreneurship starts with these seven principles:

Principle #1   Entrepreneurship is a career.

Principle #2   Successful entrepreneurs are just like you.

Principle #3   There are no secrets to success.

Principle #4   Luck is part of the equation.

Principle #5   Never reach for a gallon when you only need a quart.

Principle #6   It shouldn't only be about money.

Principle #7   Embrace fear.

Principle #1

ENTREPRENEURSHIP IS A CAREER

Who can be an entrepreneur, you ask? Anyone who wants to experience the deep, dark canyons of uncertainty and ambiguity and who wants to walk the breathtaking highlands of success. But caution—do not plan to walk the latter until you have experienced the former.

Anonymous Entrepreneur

Many of us believe that entrepreneurship means starting your own business. But that is emphasizing a single task instead of focusing on the bigger picture—much like describing acting as reading a script or engineering as building something.

All careers need to be managed, which in part involves a recognition that setbacks are inevitable, such as failing to win an audition or a bid. By viewing entrepreneurship as a career, you can more easily accept the notion that if you experience a bankruptcy, you have not failed as an entrepreneur (many highly successful entrepreneurs have experienced just such a reversal before they eventually found success) and that by preparing in advance for such a setback, you can retain enough strength and resources for a second chance.

One of the most successful entertainers and businesspersons during the past decade is Oprah Winfrey. Yet, according to biographer George Mair, she suffered a major setback in 1976 that nearly ruined her career. She had just moved to WJZ-TV in Baltimore after a successful stint as co-anchor at WTVF-TV Nashville. Unfortunately, Oprah's tenure as co-anchor in Baltimore was a bust from the very beginning. After only nine months behind the desk, she was unceremoniously yanked off the air. The station management ordered her to submit to a complete makeover, which resulted in a perm that made her hair fall out. Now bald, with low self-esteem, and saddled with the knowledge that management desperately wanted to get rid of her, Oprah clung to her career dreams as best as she could. The only bright spot was that she and her agent had been smart enough to negotiate a six-year contact with the TV station, which meant Oprah couldn't be fired without costing the station a lot of money—more than it would have cost them to find something for her to do. After the arrival of a new station manager, Oprah was offered the opportunity to co-host a morning talk-interview show. It turned out to be the perfect assignment.

As a precocious entrepreneur, Richard Branson started Virgin Records when he was barely out of his teens. Prior to that, he had failed as a Christmas tree farmer when his saplings were eaten by rabbits, as a breeder of parakeets when he had misread demand and his overstock flew the coop (actually, his mother, tired of doing the upkeep, "accidentally" left the aviary door open), and as a publisher of an alternative student periodical called *Student*, which ran articles on art, literature, and politics, along with interviews with such notables as Vanessa Redgrave, David Hockney, Jean-Paul Sartre, and Mick Jagger. Though not a financial success, the publication laid the foundation for Branson's foray into the record business by providing him with a competent staff, a functioning organization, and just enough cash to start what would become an empire.

Paris Hilton would never have had the chance to become, well, whatever she is, had her great-grandfather, Conrad Hilton, given up after two early setbacks. One of his first ventures, as an independent theatrical manager booking shows in New Mexico, lasted a single summer. Though disappointed, he was undaunted and soon after became a successful banker, but not until he had nearly lost control of the bank in a nasty, drawn-out power struggle.

Then there is Robert Mondavi Sr. In the mid-1960s, after spending twenty-three years building a family wine business, he was kicked out after a bitter dispute with his brother Peter. Knowing he was headed for a nasty legal battle, Robert Mondavi was smart enough to hire one of the best attorneys he could find and was able to prevent his brother from stripping him of much of his wealth. Instead of cursing the turn of events, Mondavi saw the break from his family as liberating. He was soon pursuing his dream: making fine wines that could compete with those from Europe.

Even Sam Walton, founder of Wal-Mart, suffered a setback or two. He had turned his very first store—a Ben Franklin franchise in Newport, Mississippi—into one of the most profitable stores in the region. However, when he signed the lease for the building that housed his store, he neglected to include a clause that would have given him the option to renew after the first five years. Seeing what a success Sam had made, when the five years was up, the landlord (who wanted to take over the thriving retail business) kicked him out. Though Sam was tough enough to negotiate compensation for the franchise rights, fixtures, and inventory, it was still a dark moment in his career:

> It really was like a nightmare. I had built the best variety store in the whole region and worked hard in the community—done everything right—and now I was being kicked out of town. It didn't seem fair. I blamed myself for ever getting suckered into such an awful lease and I was furious at the landlord. [Walton, 1992, p. 39]

But Sam Walton soon recovered, and with the money he received from the landlord started his second venture in the little town of Bentonville, Arkansas.

Perhaps no one dramatically illustrates the concept of entrepreneurship as a career better than R. H. Macy. Historian Emerson Klees (1995) claims that Macy opened and closed no fewer than six retail shops before opening his famous department store in midtown Manhattan. Each of his first three ventures in Boston—a small thread-and-needle shop, a European import mart, and a store specializing in lace and embroidery—closed within a year of opening.

Then Macy moved to Marysville, California, to open a general store. He successfully competed with at least thirty other general stores in the area by serving the needs of gold miners. However, when it became obvious, at least to Macy, that the gold was running out, he sold out and returned East with three to four thousand dollars—a nice nest egg in those days. Though his next two stores in Haverhill, Massachusetts, also failed, Macy, discouraged but with his dream still intact, moved to New York. There, with his remaining cash, he opened a small dry goods store on 6th Avenue in Manhattan. Things finally clicked, and his success brought a move to 34th Street, an annual Thanksgiving Day parade, and a "miracle."

Chapter Summary

- You should view entrepreneurship as a career. As with all careers, setbacks are inevitable.
- You will probably experience a setback before finding success as an entrepreneur.
- Successful entrepreneurs are those who can retain enough will and resources after a setback to try again.

Principle #2

SUCCESSFUL ENTREPRENEURS ARE JUST LIKE YOU

When I was young, entrepreneurs were my heroes—right up there with firemen and astronauts. I saw them as I wanted to see myself: a cocky unknown drifter, sitting down at a big-stakes poker game with the best players in town. In front of me is a stack of chips that everyone thinks won't last until the first break. Yet, with talent, guts, and sweat, I out-bet, bluff, and sometimes bully my competition into submission, leaving the table at the end of the night with a name, a smile, and a thick wad of bills in my pocket.

Instead, I discovered that under the hype, entrepreneurs are ordinary folks—someone who could be one of my teachers, a friend of the family, or a neighbor from down the street. Yet business literature continues to preach that there is an ideal entrepreneur type and that the more attributes of this ideal type that you possess, the more likely it is that you will succeed.

Anthony Iaquinto

Dozens of traits have been peddled as integral parts of the ideal entrepreneur: high levels of energy, intelligence, determination, and resourcefulness; a high degree of motivation, diligence, creativity, youthful bravado, and self-confidence; a high need for achievement, and the abilities to look at things differently, to persevere, and to make quick decisions. Successful entrepreneurs have also been said to be self-directed, outgoing, proactive, in control, hardworking, deadline-oriented, the oldest child or the only child—just to name a few. But common sense tells us that no one could possess all those attributes.

Several noted management gurus, such as Henry Mintzberg of Canada's prestigious McGill University, convincingly argue that there is no such thing as the ideal entrepreneur—that entrepreneurs display a diverse range of personality traits: gregarious or taciturn, conservative or not, analytical or intuitive; some see the big picture; others do not—in short, entrepreneurs are no different from the rest of us.

Richard Branson of Virgin has a deathly fear of public speaking. In his autobiography he shares an experience that many of us can relate to. Just as he was about to give a speech, his mind went completely blank and his mouth dry. He mumbled a few words, gave a weak smile, then gave the audience "a final inarticulate mumble, somewhere between a cough and a vomit, dropped the microphone, leaped off the podium, and disappeared into the safety of the crowd" (Branson, 1998, p. 45).

Sam Walton claimed that he was not a very organized person and rarely kept to a schedule.

Larry Ellison, of Oracle, admits to a habit of spinning funny and mostly benign stories about himself whenever he thinks reality isn't interesting enough.

Famous trial lawyer Clarence Darrow lightheartedly reflected during an interview on what he believed were the ideal traits of successful people. The interviewer said, "Most of the men I've spoken to so far attributed their success to hard work." Darrow replied:

> I guess that applies to me, too. I was brought up on a farm. One very hot day I was distributing and packing hay which a stacker was constantly dumping on top of me. By noon, I was exhausted completely. That afternoon I left the farm, never to return, and I haven't done a day of hard work since. [Fadiman, 1985, p. 157]

Even if no ideal entrepreneurial type exists, there is still a natural assumption that the more you possess of a specific trait, such as perseverance, the more likely it is that you will be a successful entrepreneur; few will argue that someone who gives in easily can be a success. However, the extremes at the "positive" end of the scale can be equally problematic. There are plenty of people who persevered to the point of burning out mentally, physically, and financially. When does "perseverance" change to "stubbornly hanging on"?

Many of the traits mentioned as being crucial for success have problems at both extremes, as illustrated in Table 2.1.

In his book *We Were Burning: Japanese Entrepreneurs and the Forging of the Electronic Age*, Bob Johnstone provides an example of the fine line between confidence and overconfidence. AT&T approved plans in 1967 to introduce Picturephone service for 1970. Managers were so convinced that the age of the Picturephone was right around the corner that they ignored a flood of negative comments from both outside and within the company. One manager noted at the time, "The whole project, no matter how doomed, will continue headlong on its course to the very end" (Johnstone, 1999, p. 182).

Findings about hazardous thought patterns of pilots that may contribute to bad judgment are intriguing (see Brechner, 1981, pp. 47–52). There may well be parallels between piloting a plane and leading a new venture.

For example, most would agree that entrepreneurs need to be optimistic, but optimism's problematic extreme—a *sense of invulnerability* (see Table 2.1)—can be hazardous. People who feel that nothing disastrous can happen to them are likely to take unnecessary chances and unwise risks. This behavior obviously has severe implications when flying an airplane or launching a company.

Being macho describes people who try to prove they are better than others by taking large risks or by exposing themselves to danger (that is, they are adrenaline junkies). Foolish head-to-head competition and irrational takeover battles may be good examples of this behavior.

Table 2.1. Problematic Extremes of Personality Traits

Undesirable Trait	Desirable Trait	Problematic Extreme
Complacent	Driven to Achieve	Overly Ambitious
Sloth-like	Energetic	Hyperactive
Unaware	Opportunity-oriented	Unfocused
Submissive	Shows initiative	Unpredictable (loose cannon)
Irresponsible	Responsible	Overly responsible (to the point of micromanaging)
Risk-averse	Unafraid of risk	Undisciplined in risk taking
Myopic	Visionary	Out of touch with reality
Pessimistic	Optimistic	Reckless (has sense of invulnerability)
Weak-kneed	Determined	Obsessed
Lacking in self-confidence	Self-confident	Overconfident
Nonconfrontational	Competitive	Macho
Weak-willed	Tenacious	Persistent beyond reason (stubbornly hangs on)
Careless, with low standards	Careful, with high standards	Perfectionistic
Dependent	Independent	Counter-dependent
Overly cautious	Prudent	Impulsive
Blind follower	Open to others' ideas	Rebellious

Facing a moment of decision, certain people feel they must do something—do anything—and do it quickly. They act *impulsively* and fail to explore the implications of their actions; they do not review alternatives before acting.

Perfectionism is the enemy of the entrepreneur. The time and cost implications of attaining perfection invariably result in the opportunity window's being slammed shut by a more decisive and nimble competitor or disappearing altogether by a leapfrog in technology.

People with a *rebellious* mentality resent control of their actions by any outside authority. The following sums up their approach: "Do not tell me what to do. No one can tell me what to do!" Contrast this thought pattern with the tendency of successful entrepreneurs to seek and use feedback to attain their goals and to improve their performance, and with their propensity to seek team members and other necessary resources to execute an opportunity.

Arrogant know-it-alls are entrepreneurs who think they have all the answers but usually have very few. To make matters worse, they often fail to recognize what they do *not* know.

An extreme and severe case of independence—*counter-dependency*—can be a limiting mind-set for entrepreneurs. Bound and determined to accomplish things all by themselves, without a particle of help from anyone, these entrepreneurs often end up accomplishing very little.

Because having too little or too much of a trait is problematic, exhibiting traits in moderation is the key to success. In other words, any average person would have the same—or even better—chance to be a successful entrepreneur as any wunderkind role model presented in the media.

A key differentiator between an entrepreneur and a wannabe is an action orientation, which can sometimes be misinterpreted as blindly moving in one direction. Action often means changing directions when things are going wrong or the market signals a change.

Young entrepreneur Michael Healey founded PC Build when he graduated from Babson College in 1995. His idea was to sell do-it-yourself computer kits. The cost would be significantly less than retail price, and using the kit would provide an educational experience for the buyer. A year into the venture, Mike was struggling. There just weren't a lot of computer hobbyists interested in building their own machine. However, Mike discovered that he had learned how to buy components efficiently, so he switched and became an IT components integrator for small-to-medium-size enterprises. He has been profitable and growing ever since.

It's important for you to understand that there are no intrinsic differences between those who are successful entrepreneurs and those who have yet to attain that goal. A venture that ends in bankruptcy could be the result of bad planning, poor decision making, market forces, or just bad luck, but not because you didn't inherently have the right stuff.

Chapter Summary

- Successful entrepreneurs are just like you.
- Bankruptcy cannot be blamed on who you are.

Principle #3

THERE ARE NO SECRETS TO SUCCESS

We've all heard that the only thing you need to accomplish something is a positive attitude. But experienced entrepreneurs know that many factors led to their success, even though the more distant from that success, the more simple and predestined it might seem. (Steve Spinelli was a very average college football player. However, every year removed from the experience, the closer he was to the NFL when he graduated!) Certainly, it's important to have a positive attitude, but it can never guarantee success.

Business authors frequently claim to have the five secrets to a successful start-up, but the five secrets of one rarely match with the five secrets of another, giving the impression that there are hundreds of secrets to success. But the fact is that decades of research have yet to find a set of universal secrets to building a sustainable business. Even such commonsense notions as providing clients with superior product quality and customer service, while significantly increasing your chances, do not guarantee success. There are companies producing products of questionable quality that have made millions. Some would argue that there are many products superior to those offered by Microsoft, yet it is one of the largest companies in the world. Although patterns sometimes appear in business venturing, each business opportunity is unique, and so are the factors that can lead to success or to bankruptcy. And that mystery is the beauty of entrepreneurship.

It is also good news for those of us who view entrepreneurship as a career because the resources, experiences, skills, and decisions that you applied to a failed business may be just what you need for your next venture. Therefore, the longer you can extend your entrepreneurial career, the greater the odds you'll be successful.

The problems Oprah Winfrey experienced at WJZ-TV Baltimore were many. First, Oprah and her more polished co-anchor were not a good mix. Second, she couldn't help being moved by the tragic stories she was reporting, and her emotions showed clearly on the screen; this put her at odds with her colleagues and management, both having been schooled in the tradition that reporters should not get emotionally involved with their stories. Finally, she would ad-lib a news story if she thought using different words from those on the teleprompter would sound more conversational. Unfortunately, the people watching the news in Baltimore did not react positively. After she had spent months in "newsroom rehab," a new station manager arrived and gave Oprah the chance to co-host a local morning talk-interview show. Most foresaw another setback, but Oprah and her co-host clicked with the first show, and that show's unstructured format and audience participation played right into the very traits that had hurt Oprah as an anchorwoman. The show was an immediate success.

Many years ago, William Durant's boundless optimism and wheeling and dealing in the markets were seen to have given him an edge in propelling General Motors past Ford Motors as the world's largest automaker. Yet those same factors are cited as the reasons he later fell short as founder and CEO of Durant Motors.

Sam Walton admitted that all the resources, experiences, and skills he had used to build a retailing empire were of no use to him when he attempted to enter the business of building shopping malls. He struggled for two years to put together a single deal, and when things got too complicated, he backed out. He later called it the worst mistake of his business career. Not surprisingly, another individual jumped into the deal and went on to develop a successful shopping center.

Chapter Summary

- There are no secrets to success.
- The resources, experiences, skills, and decisions that you applied to a failed business may be just what you need to succeed in your next venture.

Principle #4

LUCK IS PART OF THE EQUATION

> If all of us lined up, blindfolded, at rush hour, on
> the curb of the Massachusetts Turnpike with an
> offer of a million dollars if we made it across the
> roadway alive, some of us would take the risk. Most
> would be killed or injured in the attempt. The few
> who made it would swear it was talent.
>
> *Stephen Spinelli, at Babson College's Symposium*
> *for Entrepreneurship Educators*

It's been nearly taboo to suggest that good luck plays an important role in one's march to success, and anyone who believes that bad luck had a role in a venture's demise is immediately branded as a loser. "Winners create their own luck" is a favorite refrain of motivational speakers.

But luck has always been—and will always be—a part of the equation. Sports, the arts, and literature all have numerous examples where success was at least partially determined by being at the right place at the right time.

Dusty Horwitt writes in *The Washington Post* (2004, p. 7) that luck, in the shape of "inheritance, family connections, God-given talents, timing, government investments, the benefit or burden of being born to a particular set of parents (or maybe just one parent), as well as all the other twists and turns we experience," plays a significant role in determining success in most human endeavors. Michael Jordan worked hard, but much of his wealth was earned by virtue of his God-given talents, his 6-foot-6-inch height, and his advertising-friendly good looks. Warren Buffet, probably America's most successful, best-known, and well-liked investor, has attributed much of his success to his natural ability to make sound investments and his good fortune to have been born in America. Had he been born in, say, Bangladesh, Buffet's talents would have had much less value.

Zenas Block and Ian MacMillan, authors of *Corporate Venturing*, insist that luck is a component in the success or downfall of any new business development project, and they cite an example from a senior manager of an equipment-manufacturing company:

> Some managers came to me and told me that their venture had failed and that they had lost [the company] several million dollars. When I reviewed the decisions they made, I realized that in their circumstances I would have made the same decisions. They had done everything about right, but their luck ran badly and they were blindsided by an unexpected technology. [Block and MacMillan, 1993, p. 449]

Good luck for entrepreneurs can come in the form of good timing, a chance meeting, a fortunate find, or a sudden, favorable change in consumer tastes or technology. Bad luck can come through an economic recession, the death or illness of a key client or partner, a natural disaster, or unfavorable changes in technology or customer tastes (for example, bakeries and donut chains suffered during the trend to low-carb diets). In the early days of Virgin Records, founder Richard Branson nearly lost his mail-order business when postal workers suddenly went on strike.

Some might counter that if individuals are capable enough, they will foresee such bad luck. But such arguments are callous and shallow. Even large corporations, with staffs of hundreds of highly trained planners, often miss events that appear out of nowhere. No entrepreneur can anticipate all possible worst-case scenarios, develop an appropriate contingency plan for each, and still have time to manage the business. Placing blame on the entrepreneur for extraordinary events is like blaming an All-Star infielder when a sharp bouncer to short hits a pebble and veers wildly into center field.

What separates winners from losers is the ability to recognize events as good or bad luck and to possess the will and ability to act on them. In his book *Extraordinary Origins of Everyday Things*, Charles Panati (1987) points out that Edwin W. Cox was barely squeaking out a living as a door-to-door cookware salesman, so he needed a gimmick. Cox realized that one of housewives' biggest complaints was the way food stuck to pans. So, in his own kitchen, Cox developed a steel-wool pad saturated with dried soap. He soon discovered that his pads were much more popular than his cookware. Seizing on his lucky break, Cox stopped peddling cookware and went into the business of manufacturing soap pads. He named his product S.O.S. Pads.

In the late 1970s, Larry Ellison was working as the vice president of systems development for a company called Precision Instrument, which had been working on a device for storing and retrieving data that they hoped would replace microfilm readers. However, the company had neither the software to run their machines nor enough programmers to create it, so they decided to accept bids from outside the company. Seeing a great opportunity, Larry contacted two colleagues from a previous job and asked if they wanted to start a company and bid for the contract. They did and won the contract. And although the three were uncertain as to what they would do after completing the project, it eventually became Oracle.

In the case of bad luck, a successful strategy might mean recognizing that events have turned irreversibly, requiring a willingness to pull the plug on the venture in a timely manner. Unfortunately, many entrepreneurs succumb to the charms of speakers who chant,

"Real heroes never give up the fight!" But why waste efforts in a losing situation? Get out with enough resources to try again. Good poker players understand that it is just as important to know when to leave a table as when to sit down. The Japanese have a saying: "*nigeru wa kachi*—you can win by retreating." Equally intriguing is the Chinese proverb, "If you must play, decide upon three things at the start: the rules of the game, the stakes, and the quitting time." Lessons all entrepreneurs should learn.

Of course, you need to learn to distinguish between bad decisions and bad luck so you can determine where improvements can be made, but if it is bad luck that contributed to your venture's fate, understand that next time things could be very different. Acknowledging that potential can buoy spirits when it is most needed. In addition, you will confirm your collection of additional wisdom and increase the potential for success in the next deal.

There is an important addendum on the subject of luck. While it's important to recognize luck as part of the equation, it is also important that you not dwell on it. Wishing for good luck does not bring it, and wallowing in your bad luck does not lead to a quick recovery.

Entertainer George Jessel used to relate a humorous and relevant story:

> Out of work and depressed, Jessel sat with a group of friends at his club. An announcement came over the PA system that there was a telephone call for him, but Jessel made no move to respond.
>
> "Why don't you answer the phone, George?" said one of his friends. "It might be a job for you."
>
> "The way things have been going for me lately," replied Jessel gloomily, "it not only wouldn't be a job—I'd also tear my coat going into the phone booth." [Fadiman, 1985, p. 308]

Chapter Summary

- Luck plays a role in your success.
- What's important is your ability to recognize events as good or bad luck and then to have the ability and willingness to act. That reality increases the probability of success.
- If bad luck plays a role in your venture's demise, then you know

  It was probably unavoidable, which can help buoy your spirits.

  It could be different next time.

Principle #5

NEVER REACH FOR A GALLON WHEN YOU ONLY NEED A QUART

Many business writers assert that only by reaching for the stars can an entrepreneur achieve financial independence and happiness, but we argue that setting more reasonable goals can give you greater satisfaction and significantly increase your chances for success.

Just because you don't reach for the stars, doesn't mean you won't get there. Goals that build on each other are often referred to as milestones. By setting smaller, achievable milestones you will build a solid foundation that creates options, whether for sustaining a lifestyle business or for creating a larger venture.

A number of highly successful entrepreneurs had very modest goals when first starting out. In his book *Radicals & Visionaries*, Thaddeus Wawro (2000) cites Anita Roddick—the founder of The Body Shop—who opened her first store simply because she wanted a means to support herself and two daughters while her husband was on an extended trek through the Americas. It was only later that she discovered that she had stumbled onto something far greater than her original intentions.

Get Greater Satisfaction

The quest for wealth may not be as fulfilling as you expect. A research project by economist Richard Easterlin at the University of Southern California found that, after a certain point, increases in wealth improve your happiness only briefly, due to a pair of forces known as *hedonic adaptation* and *social comparison*. In other words:

the excitement of riches quickly wears off, and there's always someone who has more. Naturalist John Muir, for whom financial considerations were a minor part of life, described the paradox of wealth and happiness perfectly when he declared himself richer than magnate E. H. Harriman: "I have all the money I want and he hasn't" (Fadiman, 1985, p. 416).

There's another reason why pursuing high financial goals often leads to less satisfaction: just like in a lottery, only a very small percentage of those who try will ever hit the jackpot. If your venture does not come close to your lofty goals, you will be left with the feeling that you have failed, regretful that you had tried, and perhaps even angry that you were foolish enough to believe you had a chance. Unfortunately, disappointment, regret, and anger will not put you in the right frame of mind for a fast recovery.

These results suggest that you should only strive to reach a point where additional wealth will no longer provide you with any psychological or emotional benefits. For some, that point may come once your venture is providing you with a steady income; for others, it might mean the point when you've accumulated enough funds to pay for your children's education and your retirement; for still others, it could mean the point where you've achieved some degree of financial independence, though not necessarily great wealth.

The McDonald brothers, for instance, built from scratch an extremely successful shop in southern California and introduced numerous innovations that changed the face of the fast-food industry. But they rejected numerous offers from individuals and large companies such as Carnation to expand, simply because they were happy with what they had.

> "We couldn't spend all the money we were making," McDonald recalls. "We were . . . having a lot of fun doing what we wanted to do. [We] had always wanted financial independence, and now [we] had it." [Love, 1995, p. 23]

Increase Your Chances for Success

My most important reason for not encouraging you to aspire to great wealth is the increased risks involved in such a goal: the bigger your aspirations, the bigger the risks necessary to accomplish them. In turn, the bigger your risks, the higher the probability of bankruptcy and the greater the losses you can incur, making it much more difficult to get a second opportunity for success.

In short, why set overly ambitious goals that substantially increase your chances of being disappointed, regretful, and angry? Instead, set more modest goals that have a greater chance for success—goals that could still lead to your financial independence and will definitely make you a great deal more satisfied.

As a friend once said to me, "Never reach for a gallon when you only need a quart."

Chapter Summary

- Setting reasonable goals can give you greater satisfaction and increase your chances for success.
- Setting achievable milestones is a way of establishing a pathway to greater success, collecting knowledge and experience, and creating options for your business.

Principle #6

IT SHOULDN'T ONLY BE ABOUT MONEY

Many books argue the need to set life goals, to find purpose and direction. Without goals, we are like the proverbial ship without a rudder.

After setting goals, our next step is to find the means to achieve those goals. Some people are able to accomplish all of their life goals by following a single path. For example, those highly devoted to a spiritual or religious faith can find within it guidance and a sense of belonging, friendship, or a compatible life partner, as well as a way to express themselves artistically; sometimes they may even find a means of financial support. Other paths that can serve many of a person's life goals simultaneously are careers in medicine, civil service, grassroots activism, or entrepreneurship.

Regardless of the path, it's important to ask: What role should money play?

Unlike nonentrepreneurial careers, profit seeking must be an important goal for any venture. After all, any business that fails to turn a profit is not sustainable. However, business opportunities should not be evaluated solely on their potential to make money. In Richard Branson's book *Losing My Virginity*, he voices a sentiment that I have heard from hundreds of successful entrepreneurs:

I have never gone into any business purely to make money. If that is the sole motive, then I believe you are better off not doing it. [Branson, 1998, p. 43]

There are a number of goals that business ventures can fulfill (see Table 6.1).

When I opened my first restaurant, I had some clear financial goals, but my business also fulfilled a long-held dream of owning a bar in an exotic locale—what I called my Casablanca Syndrome—and provided me with opportunities to meet new people and build my network, opportunities I found lacking at the university where I was teaching. I also knew that being engaged in a business venture would enhance my academic career.

Though my first restaurant never became profitable, it did fulfill all my other goals. In fact, not long after I closed my first business, I was offered a tenured faculty position at a more prestigious university than where I had been employed—due, in part, to having had the experience of operating a company in Japan. I have never regretted opening my first restaurant—in fact, it turned out to be one of the best decisions I have ever made. [Anthony Iaquinto]

Many entrepreneurs who ultimately became successful made very little money with multilevel marketing opportunities such as Amway or Shaklee, but they still regard their experiences as posi-

Table 6.1. Goals a Business Venture Can Fulfill

A lifelong dream	A sense of pride and accomplishment
A need for a challenge	A longing to do something you love
A desire for financial independence	A desire to do something worthwhile
A need to contribute to your community	A need to expand your business network
A wish to expand your social network	A need for business experience
A desire to do something exciting	A hope of building a foundation for others

tive ones; their small investment showed them some of what it is like to run their own business, allowing them to collect "chunks" of experience and fine-tune their entrepreneurial mind-set.

Though only modestly financially successful, American Bryan Baird saw pursuing craft brewing in Japan as the means to fulfill two of his greatest passions: good beer and Japanese culture.

An aviation engineer and former fighter pilot named Michael Moshier set up a company to achieve his goal of manufacturing a personal flying machine. He developed two prototypes of his exoskeleton backpack aircraft, but his company failed to get additional funding and had to close. However, he still believes that someone will use his results and finish the job someday, and that will prove to him that his venture was a success.

Then there is the case of Charles Goodyear, who spent much of his career promoting the usefulness of rubber rather than seeking profit. Even though he was heavily in debt when he died, he considered his life to be a success. He wrote:

> Life should not be estimated exclusively by the standard of dollars and cents. I am not disposed to complain that I have planted and others have gathered the fruits. A man has cause for regret when he sows and no one reaps. [Klees, 1995, p. 186]

If your business succeeds in accomplishing some of your life goals, even if it is not financially successful, the experience can still be considered a positive one, and claiming even a modest victory can go a long way toward buoying your spirits.

Caution: Make sure you understand the difference between a venture that *serves* many goals and a venture that *is pursuing* many goals. While the former can be a way to sustain your career as an entrepreneur, the latter is a much more destructive path, especially if the goals pursued are in conflict. For example, it's difficult for any venture to simultaneously pursue goals of high growth and high profitability.

Chapter Summary

- Profit is an important goal for your business venture, but making money should not be your only reason for starting a business.

- If your business succeeds in accomplishing some of your life goals, even if the business is not financially successful, you can still consider it a success.

- Claiming even a modest victory can help you move on toward your next venture.

Principle #7

EMBRACE FEAR

All entrepreneurs share similar fears, such as losing current or future earnings, going deeply into debt, not doing as well as hoped, disappointing others, and losing one's self-confidence. Michael Dell admitted that at one point, he feared he was in way over his head. Andrew Grove, who titled his 1996 book *Only the Paranoid Survive*, recalled in a *Fortune* magazine article that he was so scared to leave a secure job to move to Intel that he had nightmares.

The bulk of entrepreneurship literature has long recommended dealing with fear by confrontation or by working around it. But during the dot.com boom-and-bust era of the 1990s, Americans' attitudes toward these fears went to an extreme. Young people no longer feared bankruptcy; instead, it was seen as a badge of honor! Losing $30 million in eighteen months was not only a feat worthy of attention but a ticket to greater offers.

You should never get comfortable with fear, nor should you try to conquer or ignore it. Fear is a natural reaction that you should embrace, incorporating it into your decision making and planning. You need to understand and nurture your fear. Fear is the greatest of motivators. It puts an edge on things, and when you're on edge, you work harder. New York Yankees All-Star shortstop Alex Rodriguez says that he has been consistently successful because he likes to keep a little pressure on himself. And in the movie *Cinderella Man*, it was the fear of losing his family that drove a "washed-up" boxer named James Braddock to win the world heavyweight championship. While it may be difficult to admit, without the pressure of fear, some of us are simply not motivated to act. Take this anecdote about writer Sherwood Anderson:

> Anderson's first publisher, recognizing his potential, arranged to send him a weekly check in the hope that, relieved of financial pressure, he would write more freely. After a few weeks, however, Anderson took his latest check back to the office. "It's no use," he explained. "I find it impossible to work with security staring me in the face." [Fadiman, 1985, p. 17]

Fear is also a natural defense mechanism, part of your survival instinct. Fear enables you to keep a heightened sense of awareness of the environment and so reduce the probability of being blindsided by a new competitor or a new technology. Because your business is most in danger when you're most comfortable, embracing your fear can raise the probability that your venture will be a success. There's an old saying: A rabbit that naps soundly is stew by evening.

A cautionary note about fear: it can paralyze some people. The message of this chapter is that by embracing your fears the quality of your decisions and actions will be enhanced.

Chapter Summary

- Every entrepreneur experiences fear.
- You should embrace fear because
    Fear is the greatest of motivators.
    Fear is a natural defensive mechanism.
- Your fears should be incorporated into your decision-making process.
- Fear motivates more finely tuned action.

Part Two

MAKING THE RIGHT DECISIONS

This second section introduces principles that help simplify your decision making and increase the chances that your venture will succeed, while at the same time positioning you for a second chance, in case your venture doesn't perform as hoped. The emphasis is on maximizing long-term potential by minimizing short-term risks.

This section covers these eight principles:

Principle #8 Never bet the farm.

Principle #9 Don't spend a dollar when a dime will do.

Principle #10 Always tap a bridge before crossing.

Principle #11 Only fools fly without a net.

Principle #12 Connect but protect.

Principle #13 Buddy up.

Principle #14 Learn to play the gray.

Principle #15 Plan a timely exit.

Principle #8

NEVER BET THE FARM

It's always been easy for motivational speakers to urge others to take big risks. After all, it's not their money. But for every person who risked everything and won, there are thousands who risked everything and got their butts kicked.

Why do so many entrepreneurs risk too much? Part of the reason is social pressure. There's a mistaken notion that the amount of risk one is willing to take is somehow an indication of character, that someone who took a big risk and failed is more admirable than an entrepreneur who proceeded more cautiously—and didn't lose his life's savings.

Any entrepreneur must take some risks, but taking great risks alone doesn't indicate entrepreneurial competence. Successful entrepreneurs are risk managers, not risk takers. In other words, your risks should be carefully measured against your goals, personality, experience, the nature of the opportunity, and the type of venture. For example, the more relevant experience you have, the more likely you'll be able to overcome the uncertainties of a riskier project. Indeed, experience allows you to see trends in the marketplace and make better assumptions, thus reducing the risk and *increasing* the upside. You must remember that the larger your risk, the bigger the potential fall and the more difficult the recovery.

While managing risks is an ongoing challenge for entrepreneurs, it is perhaps most critical in the early stages of your venture, when you decide what business model you will pursue. This chapter focuses on four simple rules to help shape your business idea:

1. Straightforward ideas are less risky than novel ones.

2. Even a well-traveled road has surprises.

3. Great ideas are often low-tech.

4. The execution of an idea is more important than the idea itself.

Straightforward Ideas Are Less Risky Than Novel Ones

One of the biggest misconceptions about a new venture is that it must be significantly different from current ventures in order to succeed. However, history has shown that incremental advances have a greater chance of success.

Conventional ideas are less risky than radical ones, where so much more can go awry. Michael Dell rejected revolutionary product advances in favor of incremental ones because he believed the former entailed significantly greater risks.

Management guru Henry Mintzberg proposes that a novel idea requires a greater investment of time, energy, and money to build an organization complex enough to handle its mission, as well as exceptional management skills to attract and balance the interests of investors, suppliers, customers, and employees to the unusual vision. However, it's incredibly risky to pursue such a strategy. In addition, vendors, lenders, and customers are often resistant to change, so it takes significantly more investment to get consumers to try an original idea. Committing more resources to such a task means exposure to higher risks—and a bigger fall, should the venture fail.

The dot.com crash exposed many ventures whose zeal was bigger than their competence could deliver. Boo.com cofounder Kasja Leander claimed that the fashion e-tailer of urban chic clothing would revolutionize the way we shop. The plan was to offer services in seven languages and eighteen different currencies, include a virtual dressing room so shoppers could "try on" their selections, and further flaunt its e-haughtiness by charging full prices. To achieve their lofty goals, they needed a Web site featuring complicated interactive features and a computer-animated guide—something that their technology team quickly realized was difficult, if not impossible, to build. After spending $185 million in eighteen months, the company filed for bankruptcy.

Mintzberg argues that instead of seeking the unconventional, you can find very profitable niches with relatively straightforward ideas.

In their 1992 book *Contemporary Entrepreneurs*, authors Craig Aronoff and John Ward state that Michael Benzinger, founder of Glen Ellen Wines, had a simple, yet profitable concept: sell cabernets and chardonnays for less than $10 a bottle from wine he didn't produce himself.

Michael Dell considered his venture to be a no-brainer:

> I started the business with a simple question: How can we make the process of buying a computer better? The answer was: Sell computers directly to the end customers. Eliminate the reseller's markup and pass those savings on to the customer.
>
> It didn't occur to me that others hadn't figured it out. I thought it was pretty obvious. [Dell, 1999, p. 12]

Londoner Colly Myers came up with an uncomplicated idea when he was stumped for an answer for a crossword puzzle: AQA, which stands for Any Questions Answered, will respond to nearly any query sent to it via text message. AQA replied to most questions in less than a couple of minutes—for a fee, of course.

While working on his student magazine, young Richard Branson and his colleagues surrounded themselves with music. He soon noticed that his peers spent more money buying records than they did on food and personal needs. Since the British government had recently eliminated the retail price maintenance system, he was surprised that no record shops had taken the opportunity to sell discounted records. Branson had always believed that the cost of records was too high for the people who read his magazine, and he thought he could do well enough selling cheap mail-order records through his publication. He was right and sold a lot more than even he had imagined.

Even a Well-Traveled Road Has Surprises

John D. Rockefeller said: "If you want to succeed you should strike out on new paths rather then travel the worn paths of accepted success" (Klees, 1995, p. 157). We argue that there are still a lot of good ideas and new business models yet to be discovered in old industries. Financial wizard Warren Buffet has made several fortunes betting on industries, companies, or other investments that much of the rest of the market considered too stodgy to notice.

The main reason to look for opportunities on a well-worn path is that the chances of success are considerably greater than when moving into territory in which the entrepreneur has little knowledge or experience. Buffet avoids investing in high technology because he doesn't feel he understands those types of companies.

The restaurant business is perhaps one of our oldest industries, yet there's always a new category that shows significant growth potential. Past successes included the diner, drive-ins, fast-food, and pizza delivery. The hot segment in Japan in the 1990s was casual Italian fare. In America, the latest craze is for fast, fresh, and affordable Asian food—a subset of a growing market called "fast casual."

Sometimes all it takes is one little twist to separate one venture from all the rest. Bob Wian had a modestly successful drive-in restaurant in Glendale, California, when he got a request from one of his regulars to make something more than just a hamburger. Wian concocted a double-decker sandwich that became so popular that he renamed his drive-in after it—Bob's Home of the Big Boy—and soon after, he developed a chain.

Masayuki Okano was working at his father's aging metal-mold manufacturer when he realized that more money could be earned from pressing metals than from making molds for those presses. But Okano's father was worried that if his son entered the press business, his own relationship with his existing clients would be damaged.

Okano's solution was to open a shop that would accept orders only for things that others couldn't make, usually because the problem was technologically too difficult. Those challenges fit Okano's talents perfectly, and soon he was deluged with orders.

Sherry Gottlieb started A Change of Hobbit in 1972—one of the first bookstores devoted exclusively to science fiction and fantasy—and found success by promoting a quirky atmosphere. Tuesday evenings in those early days evolved into an informal salon of young writers and editors who would sit around to discuss books, politics, and perhaps to pass a joint or two. "Everyone bought some books before leaving, but even if they hadn't, I would've kept the ritual going because the company was so much fun," she told me. Pot smoking wasn't an acceptable business practice even then, but it gave the small bookstore an eccentric image that became a major drawing card. A sign in her store read: Reality is a crutch for people who can't handle science fiction. [Anthony Iaquinto]

Tokyo discounter Don Quixote has seen exceptional growth by following a common strategy with one small deviation, which they call "compressed display." Goods are chaotically displayed from floor to ceiling to foster a treasure-hunt mentality. The plan aims to ensure that all shoppers walk away feeling that they probably overlooked something interesting, so whenever they return, they believe they will discover something new.

While Yahoo and other search engines clutter their home pages with news headlines, stock quotes, and sports scores, Sergey Brin and Larry Page set up Google with nothing more than a search box and logo. Page said:

Other companies would boast about how users spent 45 minutes on their site. We wanted people to spend a minimum amount time on Google. The faster they got their results, the more they'd use it. [Taylor, 2004]

You don't even have to come up with a new product. You can simply retarget an existing product or idea for the end market. That is, in essence, what Starbucks has done with the coffee shop and what FedEx/Kinko's is trying to do with the print shop. Arm & Hammer Baking Soda provides a useful lesson. They were able to increase sales of their mainstay product by positioning it as a carpet cleaner, litter box deodorizer, and refrigerator freshener.

People had been changing oil in their vehicles for many years before Jiffy Lube International, launched by my college football coach and some of his young, energetic players, including myself, became a national phenomenon. [Stephen Spinelli Jr.]

Great Ideas Are Often Low-Tech

Despite claims to the contrary, great successes have not always been high-tech. Dell Computers and Wal-Mart are both based on very low-tech ideas: for the former, selling computers directly to the user and, for the latter, everyday low prices, though it eventually took technology to fully implement the ideas.

Mike Dillon and Jeff Fitzsimmons set up a simple Web site to sell their Bonsai Potato Kit: Zen Without the Wait. They charged $15.99 for a pot and a 64-page pamphlet to teach you how to lovingly grow sprouts from an old potato. In their first two years of operation they racked up over $350,000 in sales. They now sell a mini-kit, which includes pruning shears, tweezers, and a 32-page guidebook, at a variety of retail outlets.

K. O. Cosmos entered the baby-shoe business in Japan in 1998 and was enjoying modest success with their handmade products. One day, a customer came in with one shoe, hoping Cosmos could make its mate. Instead, an employee suggested turning the treasured shoe into a charm by drilling a hole through the heel of the shoe and running a string through it. The client was thrilled, and ever since, the company has been busy turning used baby shoes into charms.

Another young entrepreneur in Japan simply wanted a place where his friends—mostly romantics and adventurers—would feel comfortable, so he opened a small pub that looked like a cross between a Tijuana roadhouse and a South Pacific Tiki bar. He stocked his cooler with over one hundred varieties of beer from all over the world. His hangout attracted so many, he eventually opened three more.

One of the newest entrepreneurial opportunities in the service sector is as a "clutter buster." These are people who coach others through the difficult process of organizing their work and lives. Given the increasing amounts of information and responsibilities we are facing, there appears to be a strong demand for someone to help sort things out.

The Execution of an Idea Is More Important Than the Idea Itself

In *The Portable MBA in Entrepreneurship*, William Bygrave (1997) points out that most ideas have come to more than one person—even revolutionary ideas. Darwin and Wallace each wrote a theory of evolution nearly simultaneously; Poincaré formulated a valid theory of relativity about the same time Einstein did; the integrated circuit was invented first by Jack Kilby at Texas Instruments and independently a few months later by Robert Noyce at Fairchild.

The idea may not be as important for an entrepreneur as how well it is executed. Michael Dell wasn't the only one with the idea of selling computers directly to the consumer, but arguably, he did the best job of executing that strategy. Bill Gates built Microsoft from a two-man operation by taking existing technology and overpowering the market with an innovative and skillful business strategy.

Sam Walton distanced himself from all other discounters because of the attention he put into executing his strategy. According to Harry Cunningham, who founded Kmart stores while still the CEO of S. S. Kresge, many of Sam Walton's early ideas came right from Kmart and other established discounters. Cunningham admired Sam Walton for the way he implemented and improved on those ideas. Abe Marks, another pioneer in the discount industry, commented:

> [Sam Walton] became . . . the best utilizer of information to control absentee ownerships that there's ever been. [This] gave him the ability to open as many stores as he opens, and run them as well as he runs them, and to be as profitable as he makes them [Walton, 1993, p. 110]

Much of Ray Kroc's success with McDonald's did not lie in the idea (it was the McDonald brothers' system) but in the way he implemented his strategy. Kroc believed that if you wanted to build a lasting fast-food business, the franchisor needs to keep strict control over the uniformity and quality of its service and products. He also realized that that goal could only be achieved if the franchisor is willing to sacrifice quick profits (which had, until then, been the industry's norm) in exchange for sustainable returns.

Bryan Baird has been successful selling a microbrew among the more than 250 others that have sprung up in Japan since 1994 by skillfully executing a simple strategy. The American brews a quality beer that is distinct and extremely flavorful, and he keeps expenses down by setting up shop just outside Tokyo, so the costs of doing business are lower but Japan's biggest market is still accessible.

> The Jiffy Lube concept was actually "invented" by Ed Washburn. But it was the execution of a strategy developed by Jim Hindman, my former coach, who bought Ed's idea in 1979, that transformed a small operation into a thousand-store system by the 1990s. [Stephen Spinelli Jr.]

Chapter Summary

- Don't take risks. Manage your risks.
- You can reduce the inherent risks by understanding that

    Incremental advances are less risky than revolutionary ones.

    Even a well-traveled road has surprises.

    Great ideas are often low-tech.

    The execution of an idea is often more important than the idea itself.

Principle #9

DON'T SPEND A DOLLAR WHEN A DIME WILL DO

*When it comes to control of resources . . . all I need
from a source is the ability to use the resources.
There are people who describe the ideal business as
a post office box to which people send cash.*
  Howard H. Stevenson, Harvard Business School

New Age entrepreneurship gurus preach that if you want to be a successful entrepreneur, you've got to think big right from the start. Jeffry Timmons, pioneering Babson entrepreneurship professor, tempers this. Think "big enough" is a way he tells aspiring entrepreneurs to properly assess the nature and size of the opportunity they are pursuing. An individual who turns a $5,000 investment into a thriving $5,000,000-a-year business with a significant margin can create sizeable wealth. Compare that to someone who turns a $35,000,000 investment into feed for a paper shredder.

"Going for scale" significantly increases the required investment, which increases the risk of bankruptcy and decreases the resources available to try again, if the venture performs poorly. Starting smaller is a slower path, but it's also a safer way of building both a sustainable business and a long career as an entrepreneur.

Don Laughlin landed on the Nevada side of the Colorado River in 1966 and turned a run-down eight-room hotel with twelve slot machines into a gambling empire. The dusty outpost he settled became the town of Laughlin, which now sports eight casinos hosting over five million visitors per year. His showcase hotel, The Riverside Resort, boasts over 1,400 rooms and over 1,700 slot machine, plus assorted gaming tables, showrooms, restaurants, bars—even a bowling center/theater complex.

Plenty of well-known companies have started small. Space inside Kinko's first store was reportedly so tight that founder Paul Orfalea had to roll the copier outside to make room for customers. Richard Branson's first retail record store was located in a cramped, well-worn shop above a shoe store. Ben Cohen and Jerry Greenfield delivered pints of their ice cream to local grocery stores in a beat-up VW Squareback wagon. Matsushita, maker of Pioneer and National brands, was started with the equivalent of $100 in a two-room tenement in eastern Osaka. Apple, Dell Computers, eBay, Google, Yahoo, Rohm, and Sony are other examples of highly successful companies that started out in garages, dorm rooms, or abandoned warehouses, often with just a few thousand dollars.

Of course, "small" is relative. For software developers, starting small could involve a used computer set up in a bedroom. On the other hand, a budget of $10 to $20 million was considered extremely small for Scaled Composites, the company that won the X-Prize for sending a privately funded ship into outer space.

The rest of this chapter covers three important issues:

1. How starting small can help you succeed
2. How to keep your investment small
3. Why incubators are for chickens

How Starting Small Can Help You Succeed

There are a number of ways in which starting small can help you succeed. First, it can limit the size of your mistakes. This reduces the amount of resources you need to take corrective action, thereby increasing the chances that your venture will succeed. Further, if your mistake is fatal, then the amount of money needed to close your venture will be reduced, thereby providing you with more resources to try again.

Second, starting small will force you to learn *resource parsimony*—a favorite expression of Jeffry Timmons. Having too much money allows inefficiencies to enter an operation. We have all seen entre-preneurs who, the very moment they have the cash, run off and buy things they want but don't necessarily need. This leads to the unfor-tunate behavior of solving problems with money rather than taking the time to find a solution that doesn't entail spending wads of cash. If funds are lean, then every decision you make becomes critical, forc-ing you to develop strict evaluation guidelines that can be used throughout the life of your venture. One of Sam Walton's golden rules was, "Control your expenses better than your competition." His experiences taught him that if you run an efficient operation, you can make a lot of mistakes and still be successful. Walton also believed that Wal-Mart exists to bring value to its customers, which means, among others things, saving them money:

> Every time Wal-Mart spends one dollar foolishly, it comes right out
> of our customers' pockets. Every time we save them a dollar, that puts
> us one more step ahead of the competition. [Walton, 1993, p. 12]

Boo.com became a poster child for everything that is bad about trying to start big. Boo.com burned through $185 million in eigh-teen months. In spending that much money, there are bound to be some excesses, but Boo.com took things to a new level. Besides making overly ambitious plans for its Web site, some of their ex-cesses included paying consultants $5,000 a day, plus lodging and meals, to perfect the look of Miss Boo, the Web site's computer-animated mascot. Many of their employees were given a mobile phone, a Palm hand-held device, and an American Express card. There was also a company penchant for lavish parties and seem-ingly unlimited expense accounts.

The third reason for starting small is that it can give you a com-petitive advantage. Sam Walton believes that his relatively small size in the beginning was a blessing. Because he had significantly fewer funds than the competition, he felt compelled to launch and grow his business in mostly rural areas. To the rest of the industry, Wal-Mart was a petty operator that barely registered on their radar, but it turned out that there was a lot more business in small-town America than Sam or anyone had realized, and cornering that market gave Wal-Mart a strong base, which he has used against his rivals.

Max Lapin and Alex Plotkin, founders of PhillySwirl (a frozen dessert), also discovered that while they were small, few large competitors paid them much notice. They grew slowly, but profitably. But after bagging Wal-Mart as a customer, they quickly became the target of food giant Unilever, who launched their own line of Italian ice treats similar to those produced by PhillySwirl. And while PhillySwirl has aggressively fought back, many industry experts say that Unilever's bulk and marketing prowess will eventually take its toll.

The fourth reason for starting small is that your lack of funds may force you to redirect your venture in a positive direction. Ben Cohen and Jerry Greenfield initially planned to open a bagel company, but since the equipment they needed was too expensive, they decided to focus on ice cream instead.

> I have interviewed several entrepreneurs, in such diverse markets as educational toys, greeting cards, and household gadgets, who could not afford the expense of the brick-and-mortar store so turned to alternative means of distribution, including the Internet and Tupperware-inspired home parties. All expressed a conviction that the choices forced on them turned out to be blessings in disguise, either by affording them more flexibility or by keeping their overhead low so they were able to reap higher profits. [Anthony Iaquinto]

Starting small also allows you to maintain a higher percentage of ownership. If you decide later to raise investment capital, you'll have a distinct advantage in the valuation discussion. Limiting the amount of outside investment also means that you will maintain control of your organization—something that many entrepreneurs don't realize and often later regret that they didn't.

The sixth reason for starting small is to keep shut-down costs low. If bankruptcy comes to you, the less money you spend closing operations, the more likely that you will have the resources to try again.

How to Keep Your Investment Small

Keeping your investment small begins with having the right frame of mind. You must convince yourself that you can do more with less. You must be willing to scrounge, borrow, beg, barter, or trade to get space, materials, equipment, or services.

One of the most important lessons is to invest the largest share of your scarce resources into those items most crucial to your company's success. For example, several experts have argued that if you are planning a retail venture, where location is of topmost concern, then you must make the acquisition of a favorable property your highest strategic priority. Picking a poor site just because it's cheap can be fatal. On the other hand, if you are opening a software development firm, location is not of primary importance; your priority should be on securing the right hardware to support your work or the best programmers to continue innovating.

Creativity is usually part of the discussion in the idea formulation stage of entrepreneurship. We have found at least as much creativity is needed in resource marshaling. Can you acquire the necessary resource without writing a check? Will key stakeholders help you acquire the resource—or even *provide* the resource?

After securing those items that are most important, anything else should be obtained as cheaply as possible.

Getting Space

At the beginning, you should acquire prime real estate only when it is essential to the business model (as the one noted earlier), not to support your ego. Cabletron founder Craig Benson literally started his business in a garage, cutting computer cable by hand. That business grew to several billion dollars in revenue before he sold the company.

Look for space in lower-rent districts, on side streets, or on dead-ends. If you need to make an impression when conducting interviews or making presentations, rent hotel space or use a lawyer's or accountant's office. Another option is to start your business at home, just as long as you do your homework and understand the regulations governing home businesses in your area. Keep in mind that some businesses lend themselves to being home-based, while others do not. There are a number of fine books that discuss these issues at length.

Sharing space with a compatible or complementary business may be another way to reduce your start-up costs. This is not the same as going to a business incubator (discussed later in this chapter), where you often can't pick your office mates.

Ann Olson wanted to start a relaxation center but lacked the funds to rent even the smallest of properties. One day she came across a beauty parlor that had some empty space in the back and convinced the owner to let her rent it. It turned out to be a good deal for both. Ann found a location she could afford, the shop owner received supplemental income, and each business grew by referring customers to the other.

After securing space, the next step is preparing it for business.

> I found out the hard way that you can save a lot of money by doing much of the work yourself. For my first restaurant, I hired an architect, an interior designer, and a big-time contractor, spending over $200,000. The finished product was more what they wanted than what I had dreamed. On the second restaurant, I hired a couple of small firms to do the more difficult tasks, such as the plumbing and electrical work, while my partner and I did most of the rest. The result was just as I'd imagined, one that I was proud to own, and we did it all for less than $90,000. [Anthony Iaquinto]

In preparing her first store, Anita Roddick of The Body Shop did most of the work herself. Sherry Gottlieb saved a lot of money by putting together much of A Change of Hobbitt herself. She painted her bookstore sky blue, with sponge-dabbed white clouds inside and out because she thought it would make the tiny room look bigger. The owner of a store in the same building built the bookcases for her. After getting a metal cashbox, a duplicate-form receipt book, a wicker butterfly chair from home, and a used Formica beauty-shop unit for $15 to use as a counter, she was ready for business. It cost her less than $1,500 to open her store.

We are not telling you to compromise on your vision of the business or the assets necessary to deliver value to your customers. We are suggesting that by focusing on the nature of the opportunity and minimizing and controlling resources, you have a better chance at achieving your vision.

Getting Machinery and Equipment

There are a number of things you can do to cut down on the costs of purchasing equipment.

First, instead of buying new, see what you can find at a discounter, second-hand shop, flea market, or rummage sale. You might also investigate what you can make yourself.

> In my second restaurant, we used part of my first bar's countertop to make a couple of really nice tables. [Anthony Iaquinto]

Second, you should examine carefully whether you really need specific equipment. Again, examine the key components of value for your customer. For example, some start-ups buy complex enterprise-planning software, when all they really need is a simple Excel spreadsheet.

> Don't automatically assume that you must have a computer. In the beginning it's quite possible that all you'll need is an accounting book and a calculator. [Anthony Iaquinto]

For both space and equipment, there is the option of buying or leasing. Leasing does have some benefits: it can be flexible, has some tax advantages, and can reduce the amount of initial capital that you need. That will likely lower your break-even point. To help you decide, do your research (Principle #10) and use your network (Principle #12) to make certain that you pick the option that is best for you and that you negotiate a price and contract that is favorable to you.

Don't be constrained by common practice. The Davis family started American Saw by utilizing the "third shift" in a facility that closed at 5 P.M. The owner of the building and equipment received a percentage of sales as rent. American Saw eventually grew to several hundreds of million in sales, and along the way, they slowly bought their own equipment.

Marketing

I found that most traditional forms of marketing were not an efficient use of my company's limited resources. A little guerilla marketing, word of mouth, and the spreading of flyers and business cards was a very cost-effective way of generating a consistent flow of new customers. [Anthony Iaquinto]

Many very successful Web sites have found nontraditional marketing approaches to be highly effective. For example, did you visit Google's Web site because you saw an ad or because you heard about Google from a friend or saw it described in a news story? We all know one or two little-known and somewhat out-of-the-way restaurants or boutiques that we just rave about to everyone we meet.

But if you feel that more traditional forms of marketing are needed, try to cut expenses as much as possible. For example, you might want to contact a local art school or college and see if you can't find talented students who would be willing to do the design work or the graphic arts in exchange for the experience, publicity, and a notch in their portfolio.

Finally, you should be constantly thinking about no-cost ways to market your company. For example, when Sherry G. got a phone for her bookstore, she made sure it spelled out GREAT SF. She claims that countless people over the years found her store on referral from others who didn't quite remember the store's name but remembered the telephone number.

Controlling Expenses

Controlling expenses is critical. You should commit yourself to a set of rules that will guide your behavior from the very beginning: fly only coach, stay at budget hotels, and rent only compact cars. Sam Walton controlled the amount of money spent on buying trips by instituting a rule that expenses should never exceed 1 percent of their company's purchases. Other rules could be more general, such as always looking for the most cost-effective way to do testing and analysis. Finally, be creative. When Anita Roddick opened her first Body Shop store, she cut down on packaging costs by offering discounted refills to customers who brought back their empty containers.

Richard Branson, whose alternative magazine *Student* was always a stone's throw from bankruptcy, found a novel way to increase his publication's credibility and save money at the same time. The wars in Vietnam and Biafra were the two leading issues of the day, so his publication needed to have its own reporters in both countries; *Student* didn't have the money for the flights and hotel rooms. Branson and his staff came up with the idea of choosing very young reporters, who became a story in themselves. One of the national daily newspapers paid the reporters' expenses in exchange for an exclusive story of their experiences. Both parties got what they wanted: the dailies got a compelling human interest story, and the *Student* got its reports.

Sometimes, entrepreneurs have been able to cut deals with employees.

I had a part-time cook who was planning to open up his own place across town. After a re-organization, I possessed several unneeded pieces of kitchen equipment. My part-time cook was keen on getting his hands on them for his new place, so we worked out a deal that he would put in extra hours of unpaid labor in exchange for the equipment. We were both happy. [Anthony Iaquinto]

One day, a customer came into Sherry Gottlieb's specialty bookstore, saying he loved science fiction and desperately wanted to work there. The bookstore had only been open for a couple of months, so sales didn't warrant adding even a part-timer. Unfazed, the young man said he would work for free when the owner was off, enabling the store to add hours. It was hard to pass up an offer like that, but Gottlieb couldn't let him babysit for nothing, so she made him an offer: She'd pay him 10 percent of whatever sales he made while he was working or 50 cents an hour (the current rate at that time for babysitters), whichever was greater. In spite of many days when 50 cents an hour worked out to more than 10 percent of the take, the young man worked part-time at A Change of Hobbit for the next several years.

Another rich resource you should consider tapping are members of your community who are recently retired. Some retired people need to supplement their income, and if that is the case, you must treat them with respect and pay them a fair wage.

However, I have been surprised by how often I've been approached by retirees who were simply looking to get out of the house or wanting to share their skills and experiences and were willing to do so at whatever salary I was able to pay. [Anthony Iaquinto]

Finding Initial Capital

There are several rules to follow when gathering initial capital for your venture. Here are three:

1. *Dip only modestly into your nest egg.* If you risk your entire savings on a single venture, not only will you and your family be

in dire straits if it fails, but you also limit your ability to get a second opportunity.

2. *Debt is a common source of capital for many companies*. There are times in an economic cycle that debt can be difficult to get or very easy. Don't be seduced during the easy-money times, and don't be discouraged during the difficult times. Concentrate on the reason you need the cash. If it is to buy real estate, then mortgage debt makes sense. If you can persuade a supplier to extend terms to 90 or 120 days, then trade debt can greatly enhance your working capital. Many investors in start-ups like convertible debt as a form of investing. But remember that debt must be serviced, and the financial pressures can be overwhelming. Understand your break-even and manage your debt carefully. Keep some powder dry (reserve some capacity to take on additional debt) to seize exceptional opportunities.

3. *If you need to borrow a small amount of money, try not to get it from friends or family members because there would be too much emotion tied up in the money*. This will make it very difficult for you to walk away from your venture, even when it is clear that it is failing. And your willingness and ability to walk away in a timely manner from a hopeless situation is critical for getting a second chance.

I do recommend being creative in trying to raise money for your venture. In his book *The Road Ahead*, Bill Gates relates how he and Paul Allen partially funded Microsoft with money won at late-night poker games. Babson MBA student Rezwan Shariff "raised" six figures worth of seed money for his new venture by entering and winning business plan competitions across America!

If you're not skilled in poker or writing business plans, then spend a day scrounging around the house looking for anything of value that you could sell or pawn: rare comics, bicycles, snowmobiles, jewelry, hunting rifles, golf clubs, or a used kimono. Ask yourself: Do I really need all this stuff? Am I willing to sacrifice my toys in order to pursue my dream?

If you already have a big customer, ask if that customer would be willing to pay in advance for an initial order, which might provide you with enough funds to get started. Larry Ellison and his partners invested a mere $2,000 to start Oracle (mostly for the formality of selling themselves 100,000 shares at 2 cents a share) because even before they had put the company together, they were certain of winning a big contract. This ensured that they would have enough income for at least the first year or two.

Finally, you should consider outsourcing production until you have built up enough sales to warrant the investment in a factory. Or, like Dell Computers, you can limit your investment to an assembly operation and outsource the production of parts to others. You might also be able to find a producer who will agree to share the start-up expenses by spreading the costs of any design and casting work over a period of time, rather than charging a lump sum for those services in the beginning.

Why Incubators Are for Chickens

Business incubators have been around a long time. They can be a good resource for entrepreneurs with little experience and even less funding to start a business. However, there are several reasons you shouldn't rush into one.

Poor Track Records

Business incubators have a decidedly mixed track record. While IC2 at the University of Texas at Austin has had some wonderful successes, some incubators have failed to launch even one sustainable business venture. In the most base case, an incubator can simply be a contrived real estate deal.

Make sure you check an incubator's track record thoroughly before you sign any contract, including such things as references from successful companies, the kinds, amount, and quality of services in the incubator, and references or bios on the folks running the incubator.

Tendency to Rush Things

Due to the nature of their business model, for privately funded incubators to be profitable for their investors, it's imperative that they get their companies up, running, and ready for a liquidity event (public stock sale or trade sale) as soon as possible. Eighteen to twenty-four months is an ideal time span, but even a three- or four-year period is a sprint. While eighteen months may be enough time for some ventures, others will be rushed, which significantly increases the probability of committing a fatal mistake.

If you're an entrepreneurial neophyte, rushing your business to a public offering can cause more harm than good.

May or May Not Be a Money-Saving Option

You might think that a business incubator, often touted as a money-saving option, would reduce your costs because the services incubators offer can include space, secretarial services, technical expertise, marketing strategists, counseling, legal services, accounting services, training, and so on. But these are usually part of a package deal, so it's not unusual for start-ups to pay for services they never use, either through a fee or by giving up a larger portion of equity in the venture.

Before joining any incubator, be certain it's really a cost-effective move and that you understand the consequences of giving up a large chunk of your company to outsiders.

Questionable Quality

There's a wide variability in the quality of the services offered by incubators. For example, incubators can be costly to operate, which can affect their ability to maintain a high standard of excellence in the services they offer. This is particularly true for incubators in the high-tech sector, where the pace of change is the quickest and the most complex.

Do your homework and make sure the incubator's services are high in quality and are not outdated.

May Be Distracting

The environment within incubators can be more distracting than attractive; either the silence is depressing or the noise and chaos are nerve-racking and not conducive to work.

You must ask yourself if you can work efficiently and effectively in the environment at the incubator.

May Lull You into a False Sense of Accomplishment

Many believe that if they appear successful, they will be successful, so they spend lots of money on the trappings without concentrating on what really matters: getting customers.

You need customers to build a business, not the other way around. In the beginning, you should do no more than what is absolutely needed to secure your first customers. As your customer base grows, you then develop and acquire the needed infrastructure, such as information and management systems.

May Give the Wrong Impression

All incubators have their own criteria to assess the viability of the ventures proposed to them. These criteria can vary greatly, as do the skills of those judging. This means a high probability of incubators making errors, through accepting ventures that are not really viable or rejecting those that are.

While everything might work out in the long run for the incubator, you may be given the wrong impression about the viability of your venture. You could spend significant time and money on a venture you should have passed on or regret giving up on a venture you would have been better advised to have started.

Not all incubators are equal; some are not even marginal. Carefully examine and research an incubator before signing any contracts to ensure you're not getting more hype than substance.

Chapter Summary

- Starting small can help you succeed by

    Limiting the size of your mistakes

    Teaching you fiscal responsibility

    Giving your company a competitive advantage

    Redirecting your venture in a positive direction

    Allowing you to keep a higher percentage of ownership

    Preventing you from entering into an unwise venture

    Keeping your shut-down costs low

- You can keep your investment small by

    Having the right frame of mind

    Spending what you need to on things crucial for your
    venture

    Being willing to scrounge, borrow, beg, barter, or trade

    Dipping only modestly into your nest egg

    Avoiding debt as much as possible

    Not borrowing money from relatives or friends

- Incubators are not a simple solution to new venture
  creation because

    Not all incubators have launched sustainable businesses.

    Incubators may prod you into moving too fast.

    It may be more costly to join an incubator than to go
    it alone.

    The quality of the offered services varies greatly.

    The environment within incubators can be distracting.

    You may be lulled into a false sense of accomplishment.

    You may be given the wrong impression of your venture's
    viability.

Principle #10

ALWAYS TAP A BRIDGE
BEFORE CROSSING

Some people believe that speed is the key to business success because those who move slowly are doomed to failure. So out of idealism or impatience, entrepreneurs blindly push to adopt a go-fast philosophy, often with disastrous results. Overnight successes are few and far between and mostly a public relations fantasy. Our experience tells us that most successful entrepreneurs take many years to collect the knowledge and experience required for success. Often, those who move prudently become the big winners.

Wal-Mart spent years researching the market before making an investment in Seiyu, one of Japan's largest grocery/department store chains. Then, over the next couple of years, they remained behind the scenes, carefully learning all they could about the Japanese market while slowly introducing the Wal-Mart system to their Japanese partner. In early 2004 they finally opened the first American-style Wal-Mart store, though under the Seiyu brand; that store, outside of Tokyo, has been a big hit with Japanese shoppers. Wal-Mart's prudent but successful strategy is less about staking quick claims to a territory and more about building a sustainable business.

Prudence is an essential principle for anyone who envisions entrepreneurship as a career. By choosing to be judicious, you can reduce both the number and the severity of mistakes, and so increase the chances that your venture will be a success. By being prudent, you can also minimize your losses if your venture does not proceed as planned and position yourself for another opportunity for success.

Becoming prudent is a process with five basic rules:

1. Never assume any venture is a sure thing.
2. Let someone else be the pioneer.
3. Make sure the market is ready for your idea.
4. Make sure your product and organization are ready before you start.
5. Grow no faster than your organization can handle.

Never Assume Any Venture Is a Sure Thing

Entrepreneurs tend to rationalize haste with the claim that, "It's a sure thing." But the old adage that "haste makes waste" has not lost its meaning in modern business. The Japanese have an expression: "Always tap a stone bridge before crossing." No matter how infallible an idea appears, you should always take time to make certain it is what it seems to be. Even great ideas do not spring to life fully formed; they all need testing and refinement before execution. To rush through this process invites mistakes—often tragic ones. If you want to be successful, learn to take the time to study, fine-tune, and improve your idea before you begin your new venture. And embed that behavior as a natural management process as you react to market needs and changes.

Let Someone Else Be the Pioneer

Entrepreneurs often hurry to open a business because they believe if they're not the first to market, they'll miss their big opportunity. They assume that pioneers can stake a claim, such as building a large customer base, which will give them a significant advantage over later entrants. But this strategy often works better in theory than it does in practice.

I had everything set up for my first restaurant: a group of willing investors, a design, a menu, and a cook; all I lacked was a location. I finally found space in a warehouse in Nagoya's textile district. At the time, Japan's textile industry was suffering greatly from the flood of Chinese imports and from Japan's deepest and longest recession since the 1950s. This dying district was nearly devoid of traffic after six in the evening, but it was also framed by Nagoya's main train station, its largest commercial area, and its financial district, so my instincts told me that this area was ripe for urban gentrification. I assumed that if I got there first, I could secure the best property at the cheapest price, then ride my way to the top when the expected tidal wave of yuppies flooded in. So I leased the space and opened for business.

Unfortunately, my trade in the evenings was even slower than my most conservative estimates had predicted. I was so worried about my cash flow that I spent my afternoons and early evenings standing on street corners at the edge of the district, greeting people with flyers, and trying to convince them that entering the textile district after dark was not a life-threatening proposition. After over a year of this daily routine, the evening traffic in the textile district eventually started to pick up, and so did the profitability of my restaurant.

But then, without warning, the owner of the building housing my restaurant declared bankruptcy; in the confusion of the proceedings I was asked to vacate. The losses I had incurred while pioneering the district left me with insufficient resources to relocate, and I was forced to close my business.

Not long afterwards, the textile district took off and is now the home of a new hotel, a number of boutiques, and several always-crowded restaurants; the site of my former eatery is now a successful parking lot.

My biggest mistake was ignoring this fundamental truth: The first off the line are rarely first at the end of the line. Take any race— be it athletes, horses, NASCAR, or greyhounds—early leaders seldom win; many don't even come close. Likewise, entrepreneurs who pioneer new markets are rarely still in the race when those markets become most profitable. [Anthony Iaquinto]

Sony is often regarded as the company that brought the consumer electronics industry into the transistor age, but it was another maverick—a now-defunct company called Kobe Kogyo—that produced the first commercially viable transistor in Japan.

Sam Walton didn't invent the concept of discount retailing. In his autobiography, he credits Marty Chase, founder of Ann & Hope, as the father of discounting. In 1967 Wal-Mart was generating a mere $9 million in sales from 19 stores to Kmart's $800 million in sales from 250 outlets.

While McDonald's brought much innovation to the fast-food industry, it wasn't a pioneer either. White Castle and In & Out Burger were among the many companies that were in operation before Ray Kroc started franchising McDonald's.

Apple, the original personal computer, now holds less than 10 percent of the market.

RCA built the first flat-screen TV in 1968, and Seiko of Japan was another early pioneer. But both of those companies lost out to Sharp, itself now under attack by Samsung and other Korean manufacturers.

And while today it may seem like Starbucks is the only place to get a latte, it was hardly the first company to open a chain of coffee shops.

The main drawback to being a pioneer is the significant investment in time and money involved in product design, market research, and consumer education, as well as the need to secure distribution channels and master new production processes. This increased investment does not necessarily translate into success, though it does mean the entrepreneur must assume greater risks. As we've already learned, the greater the risks you assume, the greater the probability of failure.

Had I managed to maintain enough resources to relocate my restaurant within the textile district, I would be busy seating customers right now.

It would have been more prudent for me to have pursued a less risky strategy by letting someone else spend the time, money, and energy pioneering the textile district. I could've spent my time further refining my business model: the design, menu, staff, pricing, and so forth. Then, when it looked more certain and imminent that the district would take off, I could've entered the field with a much more competitive restaurant. [Anthony Iaquinto]

Matsushita, makers of Panasonic and National brands, has pursued such a strategy vis-à-vis Sony for most of the last fifty years. As proud as Sony is in its ability to be first to market, Matsushita is equally pleased about its ability to enter markets pioneered by Sony and doing them one better. Take the videocassette recorder, for example. Even though their VCR was considered technologically superior to Matsushita's VHS system, Sony's Betamax system lost out due to Matsushita's ability to secure more movies and to tape multiple channels over multiple days. Outside of museums and collectors, the Betamax has vanished.

Make Sure the Market Is Ready for Your Idea

Windows of opportunity vary widely in size and duration. With fads (For A Day = FAD), the window of opportunity opens and shuts within a very brief time span, making it difficult for anyone to make money. For restaurants, the window of opportunity has been open for at least a thousand years and won't close in the foreseeable future, though there are better and worse times to open certain kinds of restaurants. For instance, upscale establishments usually do better when the economy is booming.

Unfortunately, many entrepreneurs, especially those with technical or scientific backgrounds, have the misguided notion that their window of opportunity is always "right now." In the euphoria of discovery, these entrepreneurs push their ideas out the door, assuming the marketplace is ready for them. They are so excited about their ideas that it's difficult for them to believe that the market wouldn't be ready.

But history is replete with good ideas that were ahead of their time:

Joseph Gayetty produced the first commercially packaged toilet paper in 1857, but his product failed because the majority of Americans at the time would not spend money on perfectly clean paper when their bathrooms and outhouses were fully stocked with yesterday's newspapers.

In 1914, a company founded by Josephine Cochrane developed the first automatic dishwashing machine. This too failed, partly due to technical problems; most homes in America did not have enough hot water to operate the machines. But they were also surprised to discover that, unlike their other chores, women of that time really enjoyed doing the dishes.

Organ maker Laurens Hammond introduced the first electronic synthesizer at the 1939 World's Fair in New York, but it never caught on. The first commercial fax machine went on sale in 1973, but it was not a success; international standards for operation weren't established until after 1980.

In the late 1990s, short-lived fashion retailer Boo.com implemented a Web site with 3-D photography and a talking saleswoman. But since most computer users at the time were connected to the Web via slow modem, browsing was an excruciatingly sluggish process, so their business quickly collapsed.

Despite tons of publicity, glowing endorsements, and high expectations, the Segway personal transportation device has yet to take off. Some believe it's simply because today's market isn't yet ready for the Segway.

The lesson here is this: Take the time to assess the market and the technology, with an emphasis on whether today's consumers are ready to accept your new product or service. That assessment could prevent a catastrophe and allow you to make a smooth transition to your next project.

Make Sure Your Product and Organization Are Ready Before You Start

We entrepreneurs are often so enthusiastic about our ideas that we make the mistake of introducing them to the market before our product or organization is really ready.

> A friend of mine opened a restaurant that she had originally envisioned as an evening establishment. But one day an adviser suggested that what the neighborhood lacked was a really good lunch place. My friend excitedly agreed and so pushed her staff to develop a lunch menu. However, instead of opting for a slow roll-out in order to work out any glitches, she decided to introduce her lunch service by offering half-price meals. As a marketing effort, it was an enormously successful ploy. Instead of the 20 or 30 customers she had anticipated, she ended up serving 135 people the first afternoon—and watched countless others going to a nearby convenience store when they saw the long lines. Operationally, however, it was a disaster. With a staff that was clearly not ready, the service was slow, the quality of the food inconsistent, and there were numerous gaffes, including misread or misplaced orders. She ended up losing many more customers than she had won over. [Anthony Iaquinto]

In the 1980s, Atari paid $21 million for the rights to produce a video game based on the movie *E.T.* But they allowed themselves only five weeks to write, produce, and ship their product to stores in time for the crucial Christmas shopping season. The finished product has been described as the worst video game ever made.

Osborne Computers was churning out ten thousand "portable" PCs a month in the 1980s and reported a 25-month backlog of orders. But when the company announced the imminent release of their second-generation computer, touted as a significant advance over the earlier model, many customers canceled their orders for the old model. Unfortunately, the release date of the new model was pushed back more than once, and faced with escalating costs and a sharp drop in sales, Osborne eventually declared bankruptcy.

Productopia, a product-review Web site, went bankrupt in 2000, due, in part at least, to their rush to create a snazzy, saleable site. Through rushing it, their product reviews were often without substance, and it wasn't clear whether they had actually performed any substantial product testing.

Never start operations until both your product and organization are ready. The simple assessment of the "right" time is when you are confident you will deliver the value you promised to the customer. We have interviewed entrepreneurs who were so ill-prepared that they had no idea how their product or service differed from that offered by their competition. Or worse, some couldn't even identify their competition. Others were ignorant of the role played by their suppliers and distributors or didn't know what government agency regulated their industry. Some had little understanding of how they were going to produce their product or made no effort to find out what technologies or processes could make their operations more efficient and effective. All of these deficiencies led to costly mistakes, many of which were fatal. But if you take the time to ensure that your products and organization are ready before you launch, you can eliminate those mistakes.

Grow No Faster Than Your Organization Can Handle

Expanding too rapidly is another common entrepreneurial mistake. Interestingly, it is exactly when business is booming that a lot of young companies get into trouble.

Growing too fast puts a lot of pressure on both your logistics and the quality of your customer service, often to the point where you're exhausting your personnel and your ability to maintain control, which can put your business at extreme risk. Even worse, expanding too quickly can burn up your cash so that you are not able to cover your bills and lead to a premature bankruptcy.

It's understandable how this can happen. It's difficult to turn away customers or new business opportunities. But you may have to do just that to increase your chances of building a sustainable business. If things appear to be getting away from you, focus on solidifying your relationships with repeat customers and focus on high-margin business. Remember, the higher the margin, the more value the customer sees in your offering.

In 1985, the then relatively small Home Depot chain plotted an aggressive growth strategy that included opening nineteen new stores. But the expansion proved to be a case of "too much too soon," and their earnings plunged. Home Depot recovered, but it taught them a lesson they never forgot.

Benefits of Being Prudent

It is always better to be prudent during your venture's early growth phase. Prudence allows you to further test your business model and gain a much clearer idea of what does and does not work. By being more judicious you put less stress on yourself and your team, so all can perform more effectively and efficiently—and give yourself the time to fill key roles with the best possible candidates. In addition, being prudent means that you can build the management, information, and distribution systems that can support faster-paced growth in the future.

You and your venture benefit by being prudent in other ways as well:

- Increased customer retention
- Higher employee morale

- Disarmed competition
- Minimized financial risk

Increased Customer Retention

It takes a lot of money and effort to attract and retain customers but only one mistake to lose them. Once you lose customers, it is almost impossible to get them back. And although every customer you gain will recommend you to three friends, every customer you lose will badmouth you to a dozen people. To compensate for the damage that one disgruntled customer can cause to your company's reputation, you need to earn the trust and loyalty of four new ones. Therefore, losing even a few customers early on can be a tremendous blow to your company's chances for success. By being careful, you can significantly reduce your mistakes and increase the number of customers you retain.

"Care" is the process of fulfilling your promise to the customer to deliver value. When Staples founder Lee Stenberg opened his company's first store, he stayed up all night putting on the finishing touches and then stayed the entire next day serving customers. "I wanted to make a point to our associates that we were going to bring value to everyone that walked into our store."

Higher Employee Morale

With any new venture, you and your organization have high levels of expectation and hope. But there are also high levels of anxiety and stress as competitors, suppliers, investors, friends, and family—and sometimes even the media—carefully watch the launch of your business. If the initial rollout of your product or service does not meet expectations, it can have serious repercussions within your organization in the form of regret, recriminations, cynicism and, ultimately, a severe loss of morale.

In Wal-Mart's early days, managers Jack Shewmaker and Ferold Arend challenged themselves to open a store in just two weeks;

though they put in a Herculean effort, the store was in terrible shape on opening day. When Sam Walton showed up, he was smart enough to simply say, "The store looks really good, guys." The managers later admitted that had he told the truth, they and their crew would have been devastated.

> Jiffy Lube founder Jim Hindman was a master at motivating employees. He believed that communicating a vision was the most important function of an entrepreneur. When the company got very large, with thousands of employees, he produced monthly videos and sent them out to all the franchisees, investors, suppliers, and employees in the field. [Stephen Spinelli Jr.]

Higher morale has an immediate impact on the viability of your venture by giving personnel, including you, the strength needed to plan and implement changes and improvements. It can also have a positive effect on your entire career as an entrepreneur. If your venture doesn't work out as planned, high morale can provide you the energy necessary to try again.

Disarmed Competition

Premature publicity aids your competitors by providing them with information that would be useful for developing a strategy and giving them time to counterattack. You should be very careful about making any announcements until you're certain that your product or service is ready to reduce the opportunities you give your competitors and increase the likelihood of your venture's success.

> Whenever one of Jiffy Lube's major competitors purchased a site, it used to erect a sign announcing its intentions and kept it up during construction. They believed they were "seeding" the market. We would saturate the immediate trade area with Jiffy Lube coupons to take out as much demand from the market as possible before the competitor opened. [Stephen Spinelli Jr.]

Minimized Financial Risk

The most important benefit of prudence is the minimization of financial losses. Being careful can reduce wasted expenditures from unnecessary or premature purchases, product returns, or poorly planned marketing; loss of revenues from losing customers or the overuse of discounts, coupons, or rebates to attract a reluctant clientele; or additional costs from the redesign of the product or production process. Being prudent financially is a natural extension of resource parsimony. When you are judiciously marshaling resources for your business, you ingrain a pattern of behavior that becomes instinctive. "If this purchase doesn't create value for the customer, then it can wait." Most important: Being prudent can prevent losses severe enough to lead to a bankruptcy.

How to Make Your Company Prudent

Being prudent isn't just an attitude. Some of the ways you can force yourself and your company to act more prudently are these:

- Question everything.
- Do your homework.
- Write things down.

Question Everything

Questioning everything forces you to take another look at what you are doing and allows you to spot weaknesses in your idea and make changes before implementation, when the costs of repairing damage would be much higher. If nothing else, taking a second glance can confirm the merits of your initial idea and afford you the confidence to move ahead. Finally, reviewing your ideas might prevent you from making the worst of mistakes: entering into a venture that you should've passed on.

An important aspect of questioning everything is to get input from trusted advisers and industry experts. One of the most valued components of being a part of a network is having a sincere and sometimes brutally honest-sounding board.

Although Wal-Mart has long been considered a leader in investing in information technology and systems, Sam Walton was just as famous within the company for questioning the need for all those expenditures. His staff felt they nearly had to risk their careers to drag Sam kicking and screaming into the information age. But Sam saw it differently:

> I always questioned everything. It was important to me to make them think that maybe the technology wasn't as good as they thought it was, or that maybe it really wasn't the end-all they promised it would be. It seems to me they try just a little harder and check into things a little bit closer if they think they might have a chance to prove me wrong. [Walton, 1993, p. 117]

Do Your Homework

A common fallacy in the literature is that the only way to learn how to be an entrepreneur is to be one. But a trial by fire leads to ashes. You cannot just jump into a venture with the assumption that you will learn as you go without making mistakes. And while it's useful to learn from your mistakes, you run the risk of making too many of them, or making fatal ones, which means that the main thing you will learn is how to file for bankruptcy.

The willingness to take time to do the homework is one aspect that differentiates entrepreneurs in Japan from those in America. American entrepreneurs are more willing to risk everything in order to get things going, while the Japanese are more likely to learn all they can before entering into a venture.

The goal of your homework is to acquire the underlying skills and knowledge needed to successfully implement your idea. This should include doing research, gathering information, and getting practical experience.

Thorough research, for example, can provide a competitive advantage to an entrepreneur.

Sportswriter Daniel G. Habib (2004) has explained how journeyman baseball player Frank Catalanotto survives in the major leagues: He takes note of every pitch he faces in order to discern any patterns, strengths, or weaknesses that an opposing pitcher may have and believes that his relentless research adds just enough points to his batting average to keep his major league career viable. It's research, not talent, that makes Catalanotto successful. Entrepreneurs need to adopt the same philosophy, especially those with small businesses.

For example, when looking for a location, don't rely solely on your real estate agent's advice. Go into the neighborhood and check traffic patterns, vehicle as well as pedestrian; ask other merchants in any prospective building about the landlord; talk to the police about local crime rates; talk to community leaders about rezoning, urban renewal, mass transit, road construction, or other potential projects that could alter the attractiveness of a particular neighborhood.

You can gather information through a variety of sources: the library, the Internet, conversations with people in the industry, potential suppliers and customers, trade associations, conferences, and conventions. Data can stimulate you and generate ideas, help you analyze your prospects, and suggest changes to your business model after you launch. But don't limit yourself to facts and opinions; you should also be getting commitments of support and planting the seeds for future sales.

Often overlooked is the need for entrepreneurs to get the appropriate experience in the industry they plan to enter. Experience is often critical to the success of a new venture. If you want to open a retail store but you have no retail experience, work for an established store for a while and study what works and what doesn't.

Sam Walton didn't just wake up one morning and decide to build the world's largest retail company. After finishing college, he wasn't sure what he wanted to do, so he took a job at J. C. Penney and soon realized that he wanted to spend the rest of his life in retail merchandising. He had also acquired the skills and knowledge to start off on his own.

Finally, you need to develop basic management skills. This can be done through a local university or vocational institute, finding a willing mentor, or from a number of well-respected civic organizations. For example, I was a member of the Fridley (Minnesota) Jaycees—an organization that promotes the development of personal, management, and leadership skills through service to others. Former Jaycees include such notables as Charles Lindbergh, presidents Bill Clinton and Gerald Ford, basketball legend Larry Bird, and Domino's founder Tom Monaghan. I learned much from my experiences as a Jaycee—lessons that have been useful throughout my career as an entrepreneur and as a college professor. [Anthony Iaquinto]

Write Things Down

Writing things down, be it a full-blown formal business plan or loosely organized ideas and notes, can help you to be prudent and careful. Organizing your notes can help you create structure and force you to think logically about many of the issues confronting your new venture. Develop a specific section for growth, laying out goals and how fast you want to achieve those goals. You should also design plans to reign in growth if it is proceeding faster than your ability to control it.

Getting things down on paper can also serve as a reality check. Sometimes an impassioned entrepreneur doesn't recognize the obvious until she reads it. For example, if your written estimates for start-up costs are $80,000, but it's clear that the most money you can raise is $20,000, it's highly probable that your business organization or your product will never be ready for the market.

Although we stress the need to write things down, don't let planning paralyze you. Doing your homework is important and should be as thorough as possible, but at some point you must act. Without action, there is no venture.

Further, action doesn't mean your homework is over. You should continue to research, gather information, and write things down. Only by continuing with your homework can you gain a better understanding of your environment and gain an advantage over your competition. As your environment changes through emerging ideas, technologies, and systems, doing your homework will keep you apace of these changes, providing you with new opportunities to enhance your position in the marketplace.

To sum up: Being prudent is a fundamental principle for anyone who sees entrepreneurship as a career. By being careful, you can minimize your mistakes and increase the likelihood that your venture will be successful. In addition, it enables you to decrease your potential losses, so if your venture fails, you will be in a position for a second chance at success.

Chapter Summary

- Winners are those who act prudently. Being prudent means
    Never assuming any venture is a sure thing
    Letting someone else be the pioneer
    Making sure the market is ready for your idea
    Making sure your product and organization are ready before you start
    Growing no faster than your organization can handle
- The benefits of being prudent are
    Increased customer retention
    Higher employee morale
    Disarmed competition
    Minimized financial risk
- You can force yourself to be prudent by
    Questioning everything
    Doing your homework
    Doing research
    Gathering information
    Getting experience
    Writing things down

Principle #11

ONLY FOOLS FLY WITHOUT A NET

I had a friend who suddenly felt driven to start his own consulting business. Flush with excitement, he immediately quit his tenured teaching position, moved to another city, rented space in an upscale neighborhood, and waited for clients to come rushing in. Unfortunately, they didn't come in fast enough, and as his debts mounted, so did the stress. Eventually, he lost everything, including his family, and the only job he could find was one for minimum wage at a loading dock. It took him months to return to any sense of normalcy, and it will be a long time, if ever, before he can get back the lifestyle he enjoyed before his poorly thought-out foray into entrepreneurship.

My friend committed several mistakes; not having a backup plan was one of the biggest. [Anthony Iaquinto]

Most of us have a backup plan in place before taking a trip, applying for graduate schools, or tackling a difficult repair job. The National Football League (NFL) and the National Collegiate Athletic Association (NCAA) understand that young people pursuing big dreams need a backup plan, so they make it difficult for college players to enter the draft before their fours years of eligibility are completed. They fear that if college players have unrestricted access to the NFL, graduation rates for football players would decrease significantly, because thousands of wannabes will neglect their studies for that one-in-a-million chance to turn pro. Although a handful may achieve that goal, the vast majority, having forfeited a promising future by not getting their degrees, will have very little else to fall back on.

At a Basketball Hall of Fame lunch in Springfield, Massachusetts, Michael Jordan asked a table full of high school students what they wanted to do as adults. Most of the young men said, "Play in the NBA." The reality was that if everyone at that lunch (about a thousand people) were a Division I college player, less than 1 percent would make it to the NBA. The other reality is that basketball careers end relatively early in life. The big question was obvious: How many of these kids prepared for the probability that their dream would not come true or that it would end far too soon?

Surprisingly, this topic rarely appears in the business literature; when it does, it tends to be adjunct to one's strategy, not an intimate part of it. Worse yet, it is sometimes derided as defeatism. But many well-respected entrepreneurs have admitted to having a backup plan when they started their business venture. In spite of Michael Dell's enthusiasm and commitment, the repercussions of quitting the University of Texas after his freshman year to spend all of his time on his new company could have been great. For instance, his parents, who were expecting him to become a doctor, would have found that completely unacceptable, so Dell came up with a backup plan:

> The University of Texas had a great program that allowed students to take a semester off with no academic penalty. That gave me the freedom to start the business without worrying about closing the door completely on my education. With that in mind, I didn't have a lot to lose. . . . if I couldn't make the business work, I could always return to my parents' original plan and go to medical school. [Dell, 1999, pp. 13–14]

The entrepreneurial process is fluid: you get an idea, forge a business model, project demand for your product or service, and launch your operations. You will make literally hundreds of assumptions along the way, and when they don't prove correct you will make adjustments. Nimbly making adjustments is a critical characteristic of entrepreneurship. Creating options and securing a safety net is a natural outgrowth of this mentality.

What a Good Backup Plan Should Do

The perfect backup plan is one that is tailored to fit your needs and situation and should accomplish the following three objectives:

1. *The plan should provide you with emotional, intellectual, and financial support during the aftermath of a failed venture.* Ideally, this will include a network of family, friends, or business associates you can rely on for assistance during a very stressful and volatile time. It should also include a process that can help you to objectively analyze what went wrong, be it simply taking time for yourself or having formal meetings with a mentor. For example, as discussed in Principle #3, it is important to know whether your venture's demise is the result of poor decision making or whether it happened because you were a victim of bad luck. Finally, your plan should include immediate financial support, perhaps by dipping into what is left of your savings or by going back to the job that your former boss said would always be waiting for you.

2. *A good backup plan should provide you a base from which to launch your next venture.* A former lieutenant in the army told me that a well-trained field officer always keeps an eye out for a fallback position—a place to which his troops can retreat if things go poorly and where they can regroup; then, when ready, they can start their offensive anew. Similarly, before an entrepreneur can try again, he or she needs time and a place to regroup; that "place" can mean a location, a new job, or simply a state of mind. The goals at this stage are to regain the will and resources to try again, to start scanning for new opportunities and, when ready, to make preparations to start a new venture.

3. *A good backup plan should make it easier for you to re-enter the marketplace.* And the plan should be flexible enough to give you

the time and the energy to complete important research and planning in a timely manner.

It's surprising how many of the people I've interviewed knew at an early age that they wanted a career in entrepreneurship but knew they wouldn't be ready to dive into it right after finishing their education. (A Gallup poll, sponsored by the Ewing Marion Kauffman Foundation, found that almost two-thirds of high school freshmen think about becoming an entrepreneur.) Using foresight, many of those people entered into careers that typically have flexible time commitments, giving them the ideal platform to pursue other business opportunities—careers such as educator, real estate agent, freelance writer, independent insurance agent, architect, dentist. If you are young or have the opportunity, you might consider moving into such a career as your first step toward your dream of becoming an entrepreneur.

Four Generic Backup Plans

There are an infinite number of potential backup plans, some as simple as having a rich and generous uncle. However, that is not under your control, so here are four generic backup plans:

1. The Weekend Entrepreneur
2. The Active Supporter
3. The Tag Team
4. The Silent Sponsor

The Weekend Entrepreneur

The most common backup plan is to keep your day job and find a way to fit the new business venture into your work schedule. One way to do that is to become a weekend entrepreneur. These individuals continue in their regular jobs and use their weekends to search for opportunities, develop and test their ideas, set up their operations, and build a customer base. This is a popular method of beginning a career in entrepreneurship in Japan and is also becoming more widespread in America. Ted and Joyce Rice started T. J. Cinnamons while still working full time. They drove a mobile bakery on the weekends to state fairs and rodeos.

Kenji Yamaguchi started a business building, repairing, and trading in customized model trains. Though he runs his venture only on the weekends, he has grown the business to the point that his net income nearly equals his salary from his day job. He is now determining whether his business is stable enough for him to take the next step—running his business full time and working part time until he feels comfortable quitting the job. By then, he should have enough cash in the bank to give him a nice safety net.

Welshman John Williams knew at a young age that someday he wanted to have his own film-production company based, oddly enough, in Japan. He also knew he wasn't going to be able to just walk off the boat, buy a bunch of cameras and celluloid, and start shooting pictures. He first found a position teaching English at a local university. He judiciously saved his money and, with the help of friends, starting shooting a series of short films during summer breaks. After several years and some positive reviews for his efforts, John and his friends founded 100MeterFilms and proceeded to shoot a low-budget feature-length film, *Firefly Dreams*. Although not a commercial success, it did win acclaim and awards at several film festivals around the world, which attracted the attention of the Japanese film industry and several large investors. Today, 100MeterFilms is involved in several projects, including their next full-length feature film, *Starfish Hotel*.

Despite his growing success, John is still hedging his bets. "I'd be crazy to give up my teaching position at this time," he admits. "Fortunes in the movie business change too quickly. I won't even consider quitting until I'm sure my company is stable enough to support me and my family."

The Active Supporter

The Active Supporter is a backup plan for entrepreneurs starting a venture with a partner. With this approach, one partner quits her job to work on the venture full time, while the other partner continues to work at his job. The partner with the monthly paycheck supports the other partner until their venture is profitable enough to provide a comfortable income for one, if not both, partners. Such an arrangement works best with a relative or spouse, but with the right agreements, it can work with a friend or business associate. Remember, expectations tend to evolve. Therefore, communication between partners in this arrangement is particularly important.

The Tag Team

Partners in a business venture can also follow a Tag Team approach—a suitable option when both partners are able and willing to work part time. With this plan, the partners work alternate periods—days or weeks—on their job and on their venture. For example, if two nurses started a senior care center, they could rotate shifts at a hospital with work at their facility. The numerous scheduling problems are usually not insurmountable. And if the venture doesn't go according to plans, the partners have part-time jobs to provide support during the period following the closing of their venture, which allows them to either move to full-time employment or start a second venture.

The Silent Sponsor

Like a silent partner, a Silent Sponsor does not play a role in managing the venture. But the silent sponsor receives an equity share by providing support to the entrepreneur rather than by investing directly in the venture. This support might come in the form of room and board rather than cash. This novel approach requires a clear understanding between the entrepreneur and the sponsor but is suitable in circumstances where such contributions are more readily available to the sponsor than cash. This approach has numerous creative incarnations. Free rent, reduced machinery and equipment lease expense, supply of product at cost—all are ways for a silent sponsor to support a venture and gain a reward.

Chapter Summary

- Before starting a business, make sure you have a backup plan.
- A good backup plan should do three things:

    Provide you with support during the aftermath of a failed venture

    Provide you with a base from which to launch your next venture

    Make re-entry into the marketplace easier
- Four generic backup plans are

    The Weekend Entrepreneur

    The Active Supporter

    The Tag Team

    The Silent Sponsor

Principle #12

CONNECT BUT PROTECT

When we hear the word *networking*, many of us picture a slick Hollywood producer who possesses a Rolodex the size of a small Ferris wheel, shaking hands with everyone he meets while throwing out insincere invitations to "do lunch." Fortunately, that isn't the typical—or most effective—network.

Like it or not, networking is something that every entrepreneur must do. Building a strong network of family, friends, and business associates can give you a competitive advantage, which improves the odds you will succeed. To help you understand some of the ins and outs of networking, this chapter covers five topics:

1. What a good network should do for you
2. What you should do for your network
3. How to evaluate your network
4. How to build your network
5. How to protect yourself from your own network

What a Good Network Should Do for You

There are, at least in theory, an infinite number of ways in which a good network can help your career in entrepreneurship—some significant, others not. A good network can

- Help you discover potential business opportunities
- Be used as a sounding board for your ideas

- Provide you with potential resources—financial, human, and intellectual
- Introduce you to potential partners, suppliers, and customers
- Be a useful source of professional expertise
- Assist you with securing space and equipment
- Give you support if things don't go according to plan

Help You Discover Potential Business Opportunities

A good network can help you find business opportunities by providing you with direct leads, by giving you advice, or by pointing you in a general direction. Ms. Takeda had spent years looking for an interesting business idea until a friend introduced her to a European craft company looking to enter the Japanese market. After visiting the company and doing some follow-up research, she negotiated for the exclusive rights to their products and is now operating three profitable stores in the Tokyo area.

Be Used as a Sounding Board for Your Ideas

One of the most important roles of your network is as an informal roundtable where ideas can be discussed, solutions offered, and guidance given. It was a friend who convinced Alfred Butts, the inventor of Scrabble, of the commercial potential of his game and the advisability of securing a copyright. Most of us have the image of the Wright Bothers secretly testing their ideas on the windswept dunes of Kitty Hawk, but the reality is that they had a strong network of advisers who helped them refine their ideas.

Provide You with Potential Resources— Financial, Human, and Intellectual

A good network should be able to provide you with a variety of resources that you don't possess and that would be impossible for you to secure on your own. This could be technical knowledge, selling skills, or familiarity with a particular region. If the people in your network are no better off than you in terms of finances, experiences, and knowledge, then your network is not useful.

> While I was going to school and not engaged in running my own business, I often took jobs in restaurants operated by family members or friends of the family. Though I had spent a year or so in the kitchen, I didn't feel qualified to cook in the restaurants I opened in Japan. Not knowing any professional cooks personally, I at first relied on want ads to locate one, but the results were unsatisfactory. So I started to build a network of people I thought would know some cooks. This included the obvious—restaurant owners—and the not-so-obvious—a restaurant reviewer from a local newspaper. Eventually, I found several great cooks, two of whom stayed with me through both restaurants. [Anthony Iaquinto]

Introduce You to Potential Partners, Suppliers, and Customers

A good network will display the willingness and the ability to introduce you to potential partners, suppliers, and customers. An example: While putting together the financing for my first restaurant, I relied heavily on a friend who recruited five silent partners. In turn, one of the silent partners introduced me to a great liquor wholesaler, another to a hardworking butcher, and still another to a supplier of kitchen equipment.

Sherry Gottlieb of A Change of Hobbit built an impressive network of science-fiction and fantasy writers, editors, and publishers, who wrote raving articles about her bookstore in newspapers and magazines, passed her name around the convention circuit, and organized highly successful autograph parties at her shop.

Be a Useful Source of Professional Expertise

A good network should also be a source for professional expertise: legal, tax, accounting, safety, insurance, and so on. In particular, your network should help with the nuts and bolts of starting your venture.

For the last several years, I have been providing advice to those who are interested in starting a business in Japan, particularly to non-Japanese. Most of the time, these people have approached me through a mutual friend or business acquaintance (interlocking networks) and want some specific advice, such as how to deal with the Japanese bureaucracy. [Anthony Iaquinto]

Assist You with Securing Space and Equipment

Having network contacts among real estate agents, shopkeepers, management companies, industry associations, and government agencies can provide you with an advantage over others in finding ideal locations at great prices. While still a fledging venture, Sony was evicted from their original location—a bombed-out department store. Desperate to find a new place that was affordable, cofounder Akio Morita turned to Iwama Kazuo—a young man from a wealthy family who was engaged to Morita's sister. It turned out that an uncle of Mr. Kazuo owned a building in Tokyo that had been unoccupied; after hearing their plea, he loaned it to Sony.

Give You Support If Things Don't Go According to Plan

Finally, a good network should be able to provide you with support—financial, emotional, and intellectual—if your venture does not go as well as you had hoped (see Principles #11 and #15).

What You Should Do for Your Network

Many people make the incorrect assumption that a network exists to serve them. Those folks tend to have their network shrink over time because others consider them a leech. The best networks are those whose "members" try to give to the network more than they take. Imagine a group of people constantly seeking to pay back a network, with interest. The spiraling benefits can be incredible.

How to Evaluate Your Network

It is important to know how to evaluate the strength of your network, so you can see if your network is providing you with a competitive advantage. This evaluation should be an ongoing process and not done in isolation; you should compare your network with those of others, especially other entrepreneurs. To review your network, ask yourself these four questions:

1. How extensive is my network?
2. How accessible is my network?
3. What is the cost of maintaining my network?
4. How reliable is my network?

How Extensive Is My Network?

Although "extent" could entail simply determining the number of contacts you have, you should also assess the strength and breadth of your network. For example, are most of your contacts from a narrowly defined field, or do their areas of expertise extend to other professions or walks of life? People with similar backgrounds and orientations are less likely to be able to give you access to new information. Also evaluate the members of your network in terms of the resources they can provide—advice, professional services, financing, technical assistance, links to potential clients or suppliers.

How Accessible Is My Network?

If you spend years building a network in one city, then suddenly move across the country, your network would become more difficult to access and therefore of less use. The methods of communication, strength of your relationships, and scheduling conflicts can also impact the accessibility of your network.

What Is the Cost of Maintaining My Network?

You must keep in contact with your network for it to be useful. For some, that requires just a card on holidays; for others, it means a weekly lunch date. In Japan, where gift-giving rituals are an integral part of maintaining a network, maintenance costs are very high.

How Reliable Is My Network?

You need to find out if you can count on the members of your network to give you sound advice in a timely manner, preferably before a crisis arises. If not, you must make your network more reliable. In addition, recent research suggests that the greater the proportion of family members in your network, the less likely that you will succeed as an entrepreneur! A possible explanation is that relatives find it difficult to offer objective advice; concerns about hurting your feelings or making you angry can suppress a desire to be candid. Therefore, if your network is composed mostly of family or close friends, you may need to expand it to include more business associates.

How to Build Your Network

After analyzing where your network is deficient, it's vital for you to build up your network. To do this, you should

- Be aggressive.
- Don't accept everyone.
- Learn where to look.

Be Aggressive

Sam Walton had a welcoming personality that attracted people. He would chat with anyone willing to shake his hand, and sometimes he would call out to people from a block away. If you have a similar gift, more power to you. If not, you'll find that aggressiveness will not come easy. Therefore, you should work within the parameters of your personality and what makes you comfortable to build up your network. For example, if you're shy about approaching somebody directly, try asking a third party to make an introduction. Then there's e-mail—often an easy way to make first contact.

After meeting a new potential member, enter the person's contact information with a note about why network membership may be desirable, as well as something personal. For example, if you've struck up a conversation about fly fishing, when you see a good article about a great fishing stream, send it along. You are "giving" to the network and finding a way to strengthen the line of communication.

Don't Accept Everyone

Despite the need to build, it's counterproductive to blindly incorporate just anyone into your network. Your network should be composed of people who can be of the most help to your business venture.

Learn Where to Look

Schools offer limitless opportunities for networking. Other excellent choices are civic organizations, fraternities, church groups, government agencies, industry associations, libraries, social clubs, and the Internet. Building ties among the business leaders in your industry is highly recommended; most will be glad to talk, as long as they believe that you are not a direct competitor. When Sherry Gottlieb opened her specialty bookstore, one of the first stops she made was to a general bookstore in the area. The owner of that store gave Sherry a number of good suggestions; in fact, after claiming that he needed more space for books in other genres, he offered to reduce the number of shelves in his store devoted to science fiction and fantasy and to refer those customers to Sherry's store.

I was able to build a strong network of business contacts through my membership in the Jaycees. Among other things, recommendations from my fellow Jaycees were instrumental in getting me into Columbia University, which laid the groundwork for all of the things I have done since. [Anthony Iaquinto]

How to Protect Yourself from Your Own Network

Virtually all business schools teach ethical behavior as a high priority and often refer to it in mission statements. This is very noble and perhaps is the right lead to making the marketplace a less hostile environment. But until this utopia arrives, you must accept the cold reality that there are a lot of people willing to do whatever it takes to get your money.

Sometimes defining unethical behavior is subjective. What is one person's injustice is another person's sound business practice, especially across cultures. The latter will insist that they have broken no laws, broken no rules. Their classic response: Don't take this knife in your back personally; it's only business.

I don't endorse the idea that you should retaliate with more unethical behavior, but you should do whatever you can to protect yourself from dishonest employees, lying customers, swindling landlords, disreputable suppliers, and ruthless competitors. Sometimes this might simply mean being a tough negotiator.

Other times, protecting yourself could entail hiring the services of a good lawyer to help you

- Protect your ideas (applying for patents, copyrights, and so on)
- Avoid abusing what legally belongs to someone else
- Write and review contacts
- Help resolve disputes among partners

Since there are numerous books available that can provide further information, I will simply state one key maxim:

> Using lawyers to prevent problems rather than resolve them is, in the long term, much cheaper and less of a headache.

Entrepreneurs can further protect themselves by following these rules:

- Don't place blind trust in anyone.
- Get all deals in writing.
- Maintain some separation.

Don't Place Blind Trust in Anyone

Although building strong relationships with suppliers, customers, employees, and others are keys to any entrepreneur's chance for success, you shouldn't go into any relationship with your eyes or mind closed to the possibility that the other party is not as sincere as he appears. For example, don't assume you're getting a great deal just because a vendor says you are.

> I know a restaurateur who felt that he and his butcher were on the best of terms. One day he visited a shop down the road—a customer of the same butcher—where he saw an invoice lying on a counter. He was shocked to see that the prices this shop was receiving were as much as 10 percent less than what the butcher had been charging him. [Anthony Iaquinto]

Katsumi Kuwabara, president of a manufacturer of boilers and water purification equipment, has had his technology stolen twice by firms he asked to manufacture his products. One of the most egregious examples (though a tad melodramatic in the telling), was an entrepreneur in Tokyo—an importer of interior décor, whose business ended when his partner ran off with his girlfriend and the contents of the company's bank account. Claude Harris—Wal-Mart's first buyer—commented that his company was lucky that Sam Walton was such a good judge of people because in the early days of the chain, it would've taken only one or two unscrupulous managers to bring the whole company to its knees.

One of the biggest mistakes you can make is paying someone the full amount in advance for work yet to be completed or for supplies yet to be delivered. There are many ways in which both parties can get what they want without one party bearing all the financial risks. That's why letters of credit were invented.

> Whenever I worked with a contractor, I negotiated to pay one-third up front, one-third when the project was completed, and the balance thirty days later. [Anthony Iaquinto]

It's amazing how many entrepreneurs, in well-meaning attempts to "build relationships," will make huge advance payments with nothing to protect them.

Don't be left holding the bag.

Get All Deals in Writing

This is still an amazingly difficult concept for most people to embrace. Some feel insulted if asked; others are too embarrassed to ask. But it's still the best way to avoid misunderstandings and disputes. Even among family, to avoid misunderstandings you should get everything on paper. Both the Kellogg and Mondavi brothers spent many years in nasty, costly legal battles when disputes got out of control.

Remember that today's best buds can be tomorrow's blood feuders. Also (and this is admittedly a bit morose) your health and the health of your partners is never assured. What happens if a tragic accident occurs and the deal is not in writing? You or your partners are left dealing with a messy estate.

Maintain Some Separation

Creating a family-like work environment has a number of benefits, including increasing worker morale, motivation, performance, job satisfaction, and retention. Unfortunately, some entrepreneurs take this concept to an extreme, forgetting that all families have a pecking order. At the top is the person with final decision-making authority, who is responsible for the family's growth, supervision, and discipline.

> One of my South American students was a part of a large family business. "You know where you are in the family hierarchy by how much cash my father gives you access to," he once said. [Stephen Spinelli Jr.]

Keeping some distance allows the boss to maintain some discipline and surveillance, both necessary to run an efficient and effective organization. But keeping a distance shouldn't be interpreted as being aloof or closed. A good boss should be responsible, sincere, transparent, and available, without letting his employees forget who they work for. Many inexperienced entrepreneurs, through sincere attempts to encourage a familial atmosphere, have become victims of the very employees they tried so hard not to abuse.

In 1970, when Richard Branson was still something of a neophyte, publishing a struggling alternative magazine for students, he came back to his office one day to find that his right-hand man, his best friend, was engineering a coup d'état. Only some quick thinking and a bold bluff kept Branson from losing control. It deeply affected him that someone he had considered family would be so willing to turn on him so quickly.

More than one entrepreneur has given employees advances on their salaries for a variety of suspect reasons ("I need to buy a new car so I can come to work" or "I need to pay off gambling debts"), only to have the employee disappear.

For a small subset of the population, taking advantage of the boss is a sport, something that people brag about at the company Christmas party or in their bowling league.

We're not advocating that you should become a tyrannical monster, but it's no fun being the sacrificial lamb either. You simply can't afford to become too nice, too thoughtful, or too accommodating. If you don't protect your business and yourself, your tenure as an entrepreneur will be brief and regrettable.

Chapter Summary

- The strength of your network can improve your chances for success.
- A good network should

    Help you discover potential business opportunities

    Be used as a sounding board for your ideas

    Provide you with potential resources—financial, human, and intellectual

    Introduce you to potential partners, suppliers, and customers

    Be a useful source of professional expertise

    Assist you with securing space and equipment

    Give you support if things don't go according to plan

- You should endeavor to contribute to, not only take, from your network.
- When reviewing your network, you should ask:

    How extensive is my network?

    How accessible is my network?

    What is the cost of maintaining my network?

    How reliable is my network?

- When building your network, you should follow these rules:

    Be aggressive.

    Don't accept everyone.

    Learn where to look.

- You can protect yourself from your network by

    Not placing blind trust in anyone

    Getting all deals in writing

    Maintaining some separation

Principle #13

BUDDY UP

People believe that if you start a company, you're the big honcho, answerable only to God and the IRS. It's not true. You must pay homage to customers, suppliers, bureaucrats, bankers, and lawyers, among others. And despite appearances, most successful business ventures cannot be attributed to the vision or actions of a single individual. Bill Gates, Akio Morita, and Steven Jobs didn't single-handedly build their companies—Microsoft, Sony, and Apple, respectively—though that's the folklore promoted by the popular press.

This chapter covers specific advice on getting a partner by asking these three questions:

1. Why is a partner needed?
2. Who should be a partner?
3. Why is it important to reach a consensus?

Why Is a Partner Needed?

Often people are attracted to a career in entrepreneurship because they think it will be a place where they can express their individuality, so the notion of a partner seems unacceptable. Even among entrepreneurs open to the idea of a partner, few will admit that they need one.

However, a partner will benefit you because

- A partner can share the risks.
- A partner can provide encouragement and support.
- Nobody can do all the work single-handedly.
- Two heads are better than one.
- There is a multiplier effect on networking (see Principle #12).
- A partner may give legitimacy to the venture.

A Partner Can Share the Risks

This is simple mathematics: If your venture needs $15,000 to get started, you can either risk the full amount yourself or get a partner who will share some of the risk. If your plans go awry, there is also a greater chance that the two of you can come up with additional funds to make the corrections; if the worst comes true, you share the costs of closing down your company, thus increasing the probability that you will have enough remaining funds to try again.

A Partner Can Provide Encouragement and Support

Partners can provide encouragement when things are difficult and support when things go wrong.

> During those awful weeks following the closing of my first restaurant, my partner and I spent many a night commiserating, consoling, and sometimes complaining about the events that had led to our venture's demise. Having someone else to share the pain not only made me feel a lot better, but we eventually fed each other's growing excitement as we prepared for the challenge of trying again. [Anthony Iaquinto]

Nobody Can Do All the Work Single-Handedly

Starting your own business is a lot of work. While that might sound incredibly obvious, it's surprising how many entrepreneurs don't realize just how difficult, tedious, and time-consuming it is. There is always far too much work for one person to handle competently. If you try to do everything yourself, you risk spreading yourself so thin that you do most everything in a mediocre fashion.

Two Heads Are Better Than One

If one partner can't see a solution, perhaps the other will. Or a suggestion proposed by one may spark a better idea from the other. One of the keys to the Wright Brothers' success was that they worked so well together.

There Is a Multiplier Effect on Networking

With two people involved, each of you can utilize your own network for the good of the venture (see Principle #12). Although your networks will undoubtedly have some overlaps, there also will be differences, so the sum of your networks will be greater than either network alone. The expansion of the network can only increase the chances of your venture's success.

Partnerships Give Legitimacy to the Venture

I know a very bright young woman who had a great idea for an alternative day care center. I thought her proposal had merit and highly recommended that she proceed, but she still faced a number of hurdles, particularly those set up by government agencies. Although she had experience running a small day care service in her home, she had never attended college, nor had she had any formal experience in the day care industry. I suggested that before she started approaching government agencies and potential investors, she find herself a managing partner with the right credentials to give her venture some credibility. She did just that and has been making great progress toward fulfilling her dream. [Anthony Iaquinto]

Who Should Be a Partner?

Don't pick someone to be your partner just because he or she is available, the first to volunteer, a relative, or a friend. One should find a partner who has a keen interest in being an entrepreneur and who has the following characteristics:

- Complement you in terms of the skills, experiences, knowledge, and personality useful for your venture (see Principle #10)
- Share your vision for your venture (see Principle #6)
- Share your willingness to play the gray (see Principle #14)

Be Your Complement

The best venture teams have been those where the partners complemented each other in terms of skills, experiences, knowledge, and personality. The best deals are those that find balance between opportunistic behavior and a more disciplined approached. If you're an optimist who always has a rosy picture of your vision, you may need a pessimist to keep your feet on the ground. If you are aggressive, always pushing the boundaries of your environment, you may need someone more conservative to keep you from popping the bubble. If you can see the big picture, you may need someone who can crunch the numbers and get all the details right.

Some of the best teams are composed of a "Ms. Outside" and a "Ms. Inside." Ms. Outside is generally the face of the organization. This person is typically sales-oriented, with great people skills—an optimist who is aggressive at making contacts, building relationships, and closing deals. She is also the one who gives the organization its vision and its energy. Ms. Inside is typically either the technical whiz or the administrative genius who remains pretty much in the shadows, but she is no less vital to the company's success. This person may also have a vision, though it's often less grandiose than her partner's, as well as an energy, though typically its output is at a slow burn compared to the intense flame of her partner. Ms. Inside is the person who turns visions into reality, the one who makes sure things get done and ensures that the organization doesn't fall apart.

Richard Branson recognized early on how important it was to have somebody at his side to compensate for his weaknesses. At *Student,* Branson had Jonny Gems. Gems knew whom the magazine should interview and why, while Branson had the ability to persuade them to agree to an interview, usually without having to give them any compensation.

Mike Wilson's biography of Larry Ellison (1997) notes that Microsoft, Apple, and Oracle have quite different cultures and products but share at least one thing in common: each matched a dynamic salesman with a technical wizard: Bill Gates with Paul Allen at Microsoft, Steve Jobs with Steve Wozniak at Apple, and Larry Ellison with Bob Miner at Oracle.

Share Your Vision

Shared vision is often assumed by partners, only to find out too late that they were wrong. Robert Mondavi Sr. believed that the very fact that he and his brother Peter had completely different visions for their wine business led to their increasing disagreements and, ultimately, acrimonious separation.

Share Your Willingness to Play the Gray

Make sure that your partner shares your willingness to play the gray (see Principle #14); otherwise, it will be a source of much friction.

Why It's Important to Reach a Consensus

Entrepreneurial ventures are often fraught with stories of spats, fights, and even lawsuits between partners. Sometimes these disputes are little more than annoyances; at other times, they can be catastrophic. Therefore, partners need to reach consensus on as many issues as possible, including company strategy, equity positions, and procedures surrounding the dissolution of the company.

Three areas that consistently cause partnership problems in a business venture are

1. Definition of roles
2. Decision-making authority
3. Allocation of resources

Definition of Roles

Sitting down and coming to agreement on partner roles is difficult because delegation often entails sensitive issues that people fear will ruin their fledging start-up before it has a chance to succeed. But if these issues are not resolved early, they often simmer underneath the congenial façade, only to explode at the most inconvenient of times, causing significant disruption and sometimes the venture's collapse.

Partner roles are frequently based on individual expertise and experiences, affinity for certain activities, or even by a roll of the dice. Generally, each of the partners will have to take on a variety of roles, at least in the early start-up period, which can make the task of assigning roles more difficult. Someone must assume those functions that none of the partners are familiar with or do not particularly want to deal with.

In addition to formal role titles and responsibilities, partners will often have distinct informal roles. In the early days of Oracle, author Mike Wilson wrote that it was considered Larry Ellison's role at Oracle to attract quality people, while it was Bob Minor's role to keep them there.

You should have a backup plan because, especially in a start-up, dynamic markets change or disaster may strike either the company or one of the partners. In the case of the death of one of the partners, all responsibilities fall to the surviving partners until a new one emerges. Many partnerships have "key person" insurance to fund the interim period from the demise of a partner to the next management arrangement. But there should also be advance agreements on roles for other crisis situations, such as when one partner is sick or injured or when there is an emergency and a partner cannot be reached. If one of the partners returns from afar, only to find that another partner has taken the company in a whole new direction, the ensuing arguments can be fatal to the company.

Roles also often need to be changed, as the venture or partners adjust themselves and their business model to the realities of the marketplace. Both partners must accept that changes in roles are a possibility, so each can be ready for it. Otherwise, you can have consensus in January and chaos in September.

Decision-Making Authority

It's a trend at business schools to introduce participatory decision-making processes into organizations to increase consensus among the members and to improve the effectiveness and the efficiency with which decisions are implemented.

In America, consensus is often defined as agreement. But it is more valuable to see consensus being made up of some permutation of agreement, understanding, and acceptance, which means there are a wide range of consensus scenarios possible. For example, the Japanese view of achieving consensus is making sure everyone understands a decision and accepts it, regardless of whether or not they agree with it. A different type of consensus is reached in the military, where attempts to reach agreement and understanding can be counterproductive; all that is necessary is for troops to accept a decision. Efficient and effective execution of tactics cannot be achieved if a leader takes the time to ensure that each soldier understands and agrees with an order.

Entrepreneurial firms need to embrace a view of consensus that emphasizes understanding and acceptance over agreement; a new venture needs someone at the top directing things. One can have equality of opinions, but when it comes to making an actual decision, someone must be more equal than others. One entrepreneur noted, "My partner has a vote, but I have two." Partners should decide who has the final decision-making authority and how that would change if disaster strikes or as the partners and their venture adjust to the marketplace.

Finding the right consensus on defining roles and decision-making authority can eliminate a major cause of friction among partners, which in turn, can improve the probability that their new venture will be a success.

Allocation of Resources

At some level, resource allocation is about running the business. Therefore, when a partnership effectively communicates decision-making authority, it also assigns responsibility for resource allocation. That should be made explicit. The person charged with making a decision about the business should either have the authority to allocate resources or a clear process to make that happen. However, once a business begins to generate free cash flow ("extra" cash flow after capital expenditures), partners often begin to seek a claim on the money that might not be in concert with the other partner's plan. Spouses can be a particularly important variable in this equation. Who gets what money for which action is an important part of partnering and of allocating resources.

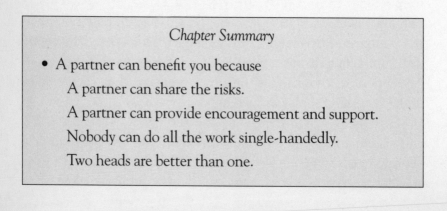

Chapter Summary

- A partner can benefit you because

  A partner can share the risks.

  A partner can provide encouragement and support.

  Nobody can do all the work single-handedly.

  Two heads are better than one.

There is a multiplier effect on networking (see
Principle #12).

Partnerships may give legitimacy to the venture.

- A good partner is one who

  Complements you in terms of the skills, experiences,
  knowledge, and personality useful for your venture (see
  Principle #10)

  Shares your vision for your venture (see Principle #6)

  Shares your willingness to play the gray (see
  Principle #14)

- Three areas that consistently cause partnership problems
  in a business venture are

  Definition of roles

  Decision-making authority

  Allocation of resources

Principle #14

LEARN TO PLAY THE GRAY

We believe that the vast majority of entrepreneurs are ethical, but the most successful entrepreneurs have learned how to play the gray; that is, they don't blatantly break rules, but they know how to maneuver inside that expansive gray area that separates the clearly established rules from the clearly unethical.

Opportunities to bend the rules usually occur in these four areas:

1. Dealing with the system
2. Building an image
3. Closing the deal
4. Being opportunistic

Dealing with the System

It is often unavoidable—and even preferable—to bend the rules when dealing with rigid bureaucracies, be they local government agencies, property management companies, or even suppliers. You shouldn't do anything illegal, but sometimes you have to get creative and display a little audacity to get what you want.

Takao Yasuda, founder of the quirky but very successful Don Quixote discount store chain in Tokyo, turned his company's maverick tendencies to bend or flaunt government regulations into a reputation with near-cult status. Responding to a 2003 shortage of pharmacists, Yasuda sold over-the-counter drugs to shoppers connected to a pharmacist via videophone. Japanese authorities ruled that this violated the pharmaceutical law requiring the physical presence of a certified pharmacist in any store that sold prescription or over-the-counter drugs. Yasuda eventually backed down, but he tried another tactic to get around the law; again, the Ministry of Health stepped in. But the public outcry over the ministry's continued intransigence forced regulators to reconsider the merits of their edicts.

> As stated earlier, my first restaurant started slowly, at least in part because I was renting space in the basement of a warehouse, which made my place difficult to see from the street. My solution was simple enough: put up a sign on the outside of the building. Although the owner of the building didn't seem to have any objections, he deferred the final decision to his management company. Having dealt with the management company in the past, I felt sure they would turn me down, so I surreptitiously obtained the proper permits and on a quiet Sunday morning rented a crane to erect the sign on the side of the building. The next time the owner stopped by for lunch, I casually pointed out my new sign. The owner complimented me on the design and said nothing else about it. The restaurant's business picked up noticeably thereafter. [Anthony Iaquinto]

When the McDonald brothers were seeking a new building design, they turned to a friend whose circus-like blueprint became a classic piece of 1950s architecture. But the building looked too flat to the brothers, so they suggested adding two arches running perpendicular to the front of the building. Their architect detested the idea and threatened to walk away from the project if the brothers insisted on keeping the arches. Not knowing any other architects, the brothers agreed to drop their idea. But when they had the final plans in hand, they immediately visited a neon sign-maker, who added the final touches: two bright yellow arches that could be seen from blocks away.

Building an Image

Entrepreneurs may find it necessary or expedient to tell an occasional half-truth in order to build their company's image. Although we don't advocate wholesale lying, sometimes a little fabrication can make the right impression. When Brian Maxwell promoted his new high-energy snack, the PowerBar, at San Francisco sports events, he wanted to make his company appear bigger than it was, so he painted a 7 on one side of the company van and an 11 on the other side to make it appear to be a fleet, rather than just one vehicle. Keiko Yamashita started her own computer consulting company in Tokyo but was worried that conservative male clients would not react positively if her business card displayed her title as CEO, so she made cards that said "Salesperson," and she eventually secured a number of significant contracts.

> When Jiffy Lube's Jim Hindman was negotiating with an investment banker in New York, he had an employee call in the middle of the meeting to say the plane was ready for the trip to the city where a major oil company was headquartered. The investment banker got the message that Hindman had options, even though no trip to the oil company headquarters was planned, and made Hindman a better offer. [Stephen Spinelli Jr.]

When Richard Branson was a teenage entrepreneur, trying to find advertisers for his struggling magazine, he would often have to use a pay phone to make his initial contact. Short on cash, he'd call the operator and politely explain that the phone had taken his coin but his call had been cut off. The operator would then make his call for him, giving him a free call: "Better still, the operator sounded like a secretary: 'I have Mr. Branson for you'" (Branson, 1998, p. 33).

Sam Walton quickly discovered the adverse consequences of being too open. One day, his company received a visit from an influential analyst from Wall Street. Sam provided her a tour of his operation, along with his son Jim, who could best be described as a casual dresser. Sam honestly explained to her, during a presentation of his company's philosophy and plans for the future, the problems they were having. Back in New York, the analyst wrote a scathing report on Wal-Mart, one that Sam Walton felt was just as unfair as it was untrue.

Closing Deals

Successful entrepreneurs know how to seal a deal. They know exactly how far they need to go and show a willingness to go there to finalize a deal under pressure. Closing is an art form, so some people are better at it than others. But there will be crucial times when an entrepreneur has to do unpleasant things, such as fulfilling entertainment requests for important clients. Sometimes, it might be necessary to overstate one's position in order to make the sale, such as the pivotal moment Bill Gates convinced IBM that Microsoft should be the one to supply Big Blue with an operating system, when, technically speaking, his company had no operating system to sell at the time.

Richard Branson quickly found out that potential advertisers were wary of paying for ads in an as-yet-unpublished student magazine. So Branson called up National Westminster Bank and told them that their main competitor, Lloyd's Bank, had agreed to take out a full-page ad. He then casually mentioned that his magazine was fast becoming the largest magazine directly targeting Britain's young people. The bank took the hook.

Being Opportunistic

Successful entrepreneurs have a knack for opportunism, recognizing an opportunity and using a little creativity or chutzpah to profit from it.

A jeweler once sent banker J. P. Morgan a lavish pearl scarf pin, along with a bill for $5,000. The next day, the jeweler received the package back from Morgan with a note that read, "I like the pin, but I don't like the price. If you will accept the enclosed check for four thousand dollars, please send back the box with the seal unbroken." The jeweler refused the check and sent away the messenger. When he later opened the box, he found that the scarf pin had been replaced with Morgan's check for $5,000.

Larry Ellison took advantage of his position inside Precision Instrument Company to make sure that the bid submitted by his newly formed company would be the lowest one. And when others in the company had reservations about the new company's ability to successfully complete the contract, he was there to convince them that it could.

Early in his career, Richard Branson invested a large sum of money in a manor outside of London and turned it into a recording studio. He hoped that its size and location would be attractive to musicians because they could stay on-site, sleeping in one of several bedrooms, and when the mood hit them, they could rush to the recording room and lay down a song. However, one neighbor was constantly lobbying the local authorities to have the manor closed down, citing late-night noise levels and other violations of local codes. It looked certain that Branson's tormentor would win, putting his nascent recording company out of business. Then Branson had a visit from two other neighbors—an elderly couple who reported that almost everyone in the area had had trouble with the same guy until the complainer asked for money; he said if they paid, he would shut up. Sensing an opportunity, Branson wired himself with a tape recorder and headed off to meet his adversary. He recorded his neighbor suggesting that if certain expenses of his were paid, he would drop his objections to the recording studio. Branson refused, and later that day, sent the would-be blackmailer a copy of the recording of their conversation, along with a note suggesting that the neighbor should withdraw his objections. Branson never heard from him again.

Finally, a wily cabinetmaker made out very well when Picasso stopped by one day to commission a wardrobe for his chateau:

To illustrate the shape and dimensions he required, he drew a hasty sketch on a sheet of paper and handed it to the craftsman.

"How much will it cost?" he asked.

"Nothing at all," replied the cabinetmaker. "Just sign the sketch." [Fadiman, 1985, p. 451]

Understanding Why Playing the Gray Is Important

Although breaking the law is unnecessarily risky, playing the gray is not. Your willingness to play the gray can actually reduce risks by giving you a competitive advantage. It also makes the most of precious resources, which not only helps your venture succeed but keeps you in a position to try again should it fail. It also hones your entrepreneurial instinct to be nimble and to see opportunity where others see obstacles.

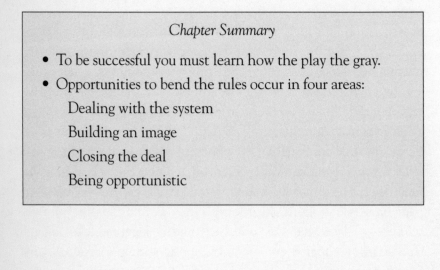

Chapter Summary

- To be successful you must learn how the play the gray.
- Opportunities to bend the rules occur in four areas:
  Dealing with the system
  Building an image
  Closing the deal
  Being opportunistic

Principle #15

PLAN A TIMELY EXIT

One of the most difficult aspects of entrepreneurship is developing the willingness and ability to get out in a timely manner—a decision that often involves even more emotion than the one to start a business. It is a rare business owner who can make a rational decision concerning the timing of his exit, but this decision can determine not only whether there will be another chance at entrepreneurial success but whether the next chapter of the founder's life will be filled with excitement and hope or sorrow and regret.

There are two distinct periods when one must consider stopping a venture:

1. Before it begins
2. After it starts

Stopping Before It Begins

As you do your homework, work on your business plan, and make other preparations, one of three things can happen: (1) you decide your idea is viable, (2) you decide it isn't, or (3) you decide the idea looks promising—for someone else.

First, you might decide that your idea is viable, that you have set the right goals and have the background and attitude necessary to make it a success.

Second, you might discover that your idea would not lead to a sustainable business, so you make the decision to not begin. Even if the venture makes economic sense but you find you do not feel passionate about it, you should still abandon it. This is often a difficult decision, especially if you have put in a significant amount of time and effort into planning the venture. But continuing to pursue a project solely through pride, impatience, or sunk cost is one of the biggest mistakes you can make. If warranted, getting out before you start means being able to use your resources for a better idea.

At one point in their career, the McDonald brothers had an idea to open a new casual diner they wanted to call The Dimer, because everything on its menu would sell for a dime or two. The brothers even planned to polish dimes every morning and give them out as change.

> But just before they were about to execute their plan, the brothers reacted to the risks inherent in a venture that took them beyond their relatively limited expertise. Their only experience with food service was with drive-ins, and with drive-ins they would stay. [Love, 1986, p. 14]

Or third, you can discover that the idea looks promising, but for someone else. It's very important for you to make those assessments honestly, for the consequences of not doing so can be severe. If you take on an ill-advised project, it will most likely end in bankruptcy. The inventors of both Monopoly and Scrabble had the opportunity to start ventures to produce and sell their games, but both elected to license their idea to an existing company with the resources and experience to make it more successful. As a result, each man became quite wealthy.

The moral: Don't let the dream of running your own business make you blind to better alternatives.

Getting Out After It Starts

We often see successful entrepreneurs as those with the knack to pick a winner, but what may be just as important is having the ability to recognize a mangy dog for what it is and the willingness to cut it loose. Unfortunately, there are no formulas to memorize, charts to plot, or benchmarks to compare that can make the decision process easy or certain.

If your venture is making only a modest profit, you must ask yourself: How long do I continue in my venture? Sometimes, if other opportunities appear, such as a job offer or a new business idea, the answer is relatively straightforward. On the other hand, the decision would be more difficult if your current venture is fulfilling most of your life goals, while a better-paying salaried position would not. In most situations, much of what determines whether your venture should be shut down or not is personal choice. For example, if your venture is making a profit that is below a threshold you have set, then it should be either sold or wound down.

It's harder to do this if you have investors. There should be ongoing discussions with investors about the future of the company. The "living dead" investment is the bane of an investor's professional existence. A minimal return might keep the founder in a comfortable position but allows no opportunity for a return on investors' money. Winding down the company might get some capital returned to investors and allow for a tax write-off.

Even if your company is highly profitable, you may need to consider an exit if you can see disaster on the horizon in the form of unfavorable changes in government regulations, technology, or consumer tastes. Making this decision is difficult, but if you are able to make it in a timely way, you will significantly increase the probability of having a second chance at finding a sustainable business. "I made my money selling too early," said famed investor Bernard Baruch.

Finally, if both your profit-and-loss statement and your balance sheet look grim, it doesn't mean your company is failing. Business ventures often go through dark times during their early stages. A loss may simply mean that your idea just hasn't caught on yet or that your projections were inaccurate and you need to make some adjustments to your business model. In this case you need to ask two important questions:

1. Can changes be made?
2. Will these changes lead to a significant increase in performance?

If you can confidently answer yes to each of those questions, then you can define your venture as still having potential. However, if the red ink continues to flow after the changes have been made, then you must ask: How much money am I willing to lose? If your venture starts to drain cash from your personal finances, then it is time to seriously consider shutting it down, as the longer you wait, the fewer resources you will have to make a quick recovery.

To keep yourself from losing too much, set a lower limit right from the start. This should be an amount that you can lose without putting yourself and your family in financial difficulties and that will not threaten your ability to try again.

Unfortunately, when businesses go south, too many entrepreneurs remain in a state of denial. They refuse either to recognize or to admit that their venture is failing; they make themselves believe that each new day will be different from the rest. But most often, each new day does not produce what these entrepreneurs so earnestly work for and so desperately hope for. They hang on because they have projected too much of themselves into their project, so it's as if, by killing their business, they are committing suicide.

To make a timely exit, you must maintain some separation between you and your business. Try to salvage as much as you can before it is too late. It is illogical to fight to the death; by doing so, you waste valuable effort and resources.

Chapter Summary

- There are two distinct periods when one must consider stopping a venture:

  Before it begins, when you decide: (1) your idea is viable, that you have set the right goals and have the background and attitude necessary to make it a success; (2) your idea would not lead to a sustainable business, so you make the decision to not begin; (3) you discover that the idea looks promising, but for someone else

  After it starts, when the ability and willingness to execute a timely exit is crucial to getting a second chance at success

FINAL WORDS

In *Never Bet the Farm*, we celebrate entrepreneurship in its entirety and present a framework that can help entrepreneurs reduce risks and simplify decision making.

We contend that what separates winners from losers is not bankruptcy (many entrepreneurs experience such a catastrophe or something just short of bankruptcy) but the ability that winners have to keep themselves in the game by maintaining enough will and resources to try again. As someone once said, "Great football players are not judged by how many times they are tackled but rather how many times they get up!"

It has also been said that the best time to respond to a disaster is before it occurs. In *Never Bet the Farm*, we present a proactive approach to business failure. By following the principles in this book, you will be prepared for the worst so you can limit any damage and preserve assets to try again. Finally, by being ready for a catastrophe, you could prevent the very thing you fear most: business failure.

We hope *Never Bet the Farm* has been both enlightening and useful. We wish you the very best of luck as you pursue your career in entrepreneurship.

If you would like to share a comment or anecdote, please write us at: neverbetthefarm@hotmail.com.

An Entrepreneur's Guidebook

Whether you are a neophyte or an experienced entrepreneur, we argue in this book that you need to have the right frame of mind to be successful. In addition, you must make the right decisions in such areas as finding the right opportunity (Principle #8), building a strong network (Principle #10), doing your homework (Principle #12), and finding a good partner (Principle #13). To assist you, we present three useful resources.

University Centers

The first resource is a list of over five hundred universities and colleges around the world that maintain a center or program devoted to entrepreneurship. Although the vast majority of these centers are affiliated with a business school, some are attached to a law or engineering school, such as the University of Pennsylvania Law School's Small Business Clinic.

Many of the centers listed offer entrepreneurs free or low-cost consulting. Other services provided vary from a "Tip of the Month," which you can view on the Web site of the Jim Moran Institute for Global Entrepreneurship at Florida State University, to breakfast seminars offered by Black Hills State University's Center for Business and Entrepreneurship, to a faith-based entrepreneurship program at Huntington College. Other offerings include workshops, business plan contests, incubators, newsletters, online magazines, online libraries, books, articles, periodicals, and a variety of social events. Finally, nearly all of these centers maintain links to other organizations, such as the U.S. Small Business Administration, the Kauffman Foundation, and local chambers of commerce.

Selected Web Sites

The second resource consists of a list of Web sites focusing on national business organizations and government agencies. We also provide examples of Web sites sponsored by local organizations and would encourage you to search for similar organizations in your home town. At the end of this section we present a list of relevant online business publications.

Selected Books

In the third resource you will find a list of entrepreneurship-related books, categorized into sections such as "Textbooks and How-To Books," "Finance," and "E-business." Most of these books are available online or at your local bookstore, although for some, you'll have to make a trip to your local library.

We have not limited the resources in this section to those based in the United States for several reasons. First, even very small businesses are part of the growing global marketplace, and networking internationally can expand your list of potential customers, suppliers, and investors. Second, great ideas in products, services, processes, or management methods are not limited to institutions in the United States. Finally, there are an increasing number of entrepreneurial opportunities for individuals overseas.

UNIVERSITY CENTERS

Alabama

Alabama State University
Small Business Development Center
915 South Jackson St.
Montgomery, AL 36101
334-229-4138
www.cobanetwork.com/sbdc

Auburn University
Lowder Center for Family Business
   and Entrepreneurship
700 Pelham Rd., Room 105
334-844-2266
www.business.auburn.edu

Troy State University
Small Business Development Center
102 Bibb Graves Hall
Troy, AL 36082
334-670-3771
http://www.troy.edu

University of Alabama
Small Business Development Center
P.O. Box 870397
Tuscaloosa, AL 35487
205-348-7011
phaninen@cba.ua.edu
www.cba.ua.edu

Auburn University
Small Business Development Center
415 W. Magnolia
Auburn University, AL 36849
334-844-2352
www.business.auburn.edu/
   programs/sbdc

Jacksonville State University
Small Business Development Center
Lowder Building
256-782-5271
sbdc@jsu.edu
www.jsu.edu/depart/sbdc

University of Alabama
Alabama Data Center
P.O. Box 870221
Tuscaloosa, AL 35487
205-348-6191
www.cba.ua.edu

University of Alabama
Family Business Forum
P.O. Box 870221
Tuscaloosa, AL 35487
205-348-7270
http://fbf.cba.ua.edu

University of Alabama, Birmingham
Small Business Development Center
1055 11th St., Room 202
Birmingham, AL 35294
205-934-6760
www.una.edu/sbdc

University of South Alabama
Small Business Development Center
Mitchell College of Business
307 University Blvd.
Mobile, AL 36688
251-460-6902
www.usouthal.edu

University of North Alabama
Small Business Development Center
Florence, AL 35632
256-765-4405
www.business.uab.edu/sbdc

The University of West Alabama
Small Business Development Center
Station 35
Livingston, AL 35470
205-652-3665
www.uwa.edu

Alaska

University of Alaska, Anchorage
Small Business Development Center
430 W. 7th St., Suite 110
Anchorage, AK 99508-8060
907-274-7232
www.uaa.alaska.edu

University of Alaska, Southeast
Small Business Management
   Program
11120 Glacier Hwy.
Juneau, AK 99801
907-465-6350
1-877-465-4827, ext. 6350
www.uas.alaska.edu/business

Other offices:
  Fairbanks 907-4456-7232
  Kenai Peninsula 907-262-7497
  Ketchikan 907-225-1388
  Matanuska Susitna Valley
    907-373-7232

Arizona

Arizona State University
The Center for the Advancement
   of Small Business
W. P. Carey School of Business
Tempe, AZ 85287
480-965-3962
smallbiz@asu.edu
www.wpcarey.asu.edu/seid/casb

Arizona Western College
Small Business Development Center
281 West 24th St.
Yuma, AZ
928-341-1650

Coconino Community College
Small Business Development Center
3000 N. Fourth St.
Flagstaff, AZ 86004
928-526-7653

Central Arizona College
Small Business Development Center
1015 E. Florence, Suite B
Casa Grande, AZ 85222
520-426-4341
SBDC@centralaz.edu
www.cac.cc.az.us/biz

Eastern Arizona College
Small Business Development Center
615 N. Stadium
Thatcher, AZ 85552
9298-428-8590
www.eac.edu

Gila Community College
Small Business Development Center
Globe, AZ
928-425-8481

Maricopa Community College
Small Business Development Center
2400 N. Central Ave., Suite 104
Phoenix, AZ 85004
480-784-0590
www.maricopa.edu

Mohave Community College
Small Business Development Center
1971 Jagerson
Kingman, AZ 86401
928-757-0895
www.mohave.edu

Northern Arizona University
The Small Business Institute
Center for Business Outreach
NAU Box 15066
928-523-3322
www.cba.nau.edu/business/bocho

The University of Arizona
McGuire Entrepreneurship Program
Eller College of Management
McClelland Hall 202
520-626-5269
entre.net@eller.arizona.edu
http://entrepreneurship.eller.
    arizona.edu

Pima Community College
Small Business Development Center
401 No. Bonita Ave.
Tucson, AZ 85709
520-206-6404
sbdc@pimacc.pima.edu
www.cc.pima.edu

Yavapai College
Small Business Development Center
1100 E. Sheldon St.
Prescott, AZ 6912
928-776-2008
www.yavapai.cc.az.us

Arkansas

Arkansas State University
Small Business Development Center
College of Business, Room 119A
Jonesboro, AR 72467
870-972-3517
www.deltaced.astate.edu/asbdc.htm

Southern Arkansas University
Small Business Development Center
College of Business
P.O. Box 9192
870-235-5023
www.saumag.edu

University of Arkansas, Fort Smith
Small Business Development Center
Business and Professional Institute
College of Business
Fort Smith, AR 72913
479-788-7758
www.uafortsmith.edu/SBDC

University of Arkansas, Little Rock
Small Business Development Center
2801 S. University
Little Rock, AR 72204
501-324-9043
www.asbdc.ualr.edu

Henderson State University
Small Business Development Center
P.O. Box 7624
Arkadelphia, AR 71999
870-230-5224
www.hsu.edu/sbdc

University of Arkansas Fayetteville
Small Business Development Center
Donald W. Reynolds Center,
   Suite 140
Sam M. Walton College of Business
479-575-5148
http://waltoncollege.uark.edu

University of Arkansas, Monticello
Small Business Development Center
1609 East Ash
McGehee, AR 71654
870-222-4900
www.uamont.edu

California

California Polytechnic State
   University, San Luis Obispo
California Central Coast Research
   Small Business Institute
   Partnership
San Luis Obispo, CA 93407
www.c3rp.org

California Polytechnic State
   University, San Luis Obispo
Orfalea College of Business
One Grand Avenue
San Luis Obispo, CA 93407
805-756-2704
www.calpoly.edu

California State University,
  Bakersfield
Family Business Institute/Small
  Business Library
Business Research and Education
  Center
9001 Stockdale Hwy.
Bakersfield, CA 93311
661-664-2435
www.csubak.edu/brec

California State University, Fresno
Institute for Developing
  Entrepreneurial Action
Sid Craig School of Business
5245 N. Backer Ave.
Fresno, CA 93740
559-278-2841
www.craig.csufresno.edu

California State University, Fullerton
Center for Entrepreneurship
College of Business and Economics
Fullerton, CA 92834
714-278-4652
sbiame@fullerton.edu
www.fullerton.edu

California State University,
  Los Angeles
Entrepreneurship Institute
College of Business and Economics
Los Angeles, CA 90032
323-343-2800
http://cbe.calstatela.edu

California State University, Chico
Center for Entrepreneurship
College of Business
Tehama Hall
Chico, CA 95929
530-898-6271
bus@csuchico.edu
www.cob.csuchico.edu

California State University, Fresno
Small Business Development Center
1901 E. Shields, Suite 202
Fresno, CA 93740
559-230-4056
www.ccsbdc.org

California State University,
  Hayward
Department of Marketing and
  and Entrepreneurship
College of Business and Economics
Hayward, CA 94542
www.csuhayward.edu

California State University,
  Northridge
Wells Fargo Center for Small
  Business and Entrepreneurship
Northridge, CA 91330
818-677-6646
wfcsbe@csun.edu
www.csun.edu/wfcsbe

California State University,
Northridge
Family Business Center
College of Business Administration
and Economics
Northridge, CA 91330
818-677-4612
http://www.csun.edu

California State University,
San Bernardino
Inland Empire Center for
Entrepreneurship
5500 University Pkwy.
San Bernardino, CA 92407
909-880-5000
www.csusb.edu

Claremont Graduate University
The Venture Finance Institute
Peter F. Drucker Graduate School
of Management
1021 N. Dartmouth
Claremont, CA 91711
909-607-3310
http://vfi.cgu.edu

National University
The Women's Business Center
of California
619-563-7118
wbccinfo@natuniv.edu
www.nu.edu/Academics/
Schools/SOBM/Wbcc.html

San Francisco State University
Ohrenschall Center for
Entrepreneurship
College of Business
1600 Holloway Ave.
San Francisco, CA 94132
415-338-7886
www.sfsu.edu/~cfe

California State University,
Sacramento
Center for Small Business
College of Business Administration
Sacramento, CA 95819
916-278-7278
http://cbaweb.cba.csus.edu/csb

Chapman University
Ralph L. Leatherby Center for
Entrepreneurship and Ethics
The George L. Argyros School
of Business and Economics
Orange, CA 92866
714-997-6815
www.chapman.edu/argyros/
asbecenters

Loyola Marymount University
Center for Entrepreneurship
Program
College of Business Administration
Los Angeles, CA 90045
310-338-2700
www.lmu.edu/pages/118.asp

San Diego State University
Entrepreneurial Management
Center
College of Business Administration
5250 Campanile Dr.
San Diego, CA 92182
619-594-2781
www.sdsu.edu

Santa Clara University
Center for Innovation and
Entrepreneurship
Leavy School of Business
Santa Clara, CA 95053
408-554-5757
innovation@scv.edu
http://business.scu.edu/CIE/main

Stanford University
Center for Entrepreneurial Studies
Graduate School of Business
Stanford, CA 94305
ces@gsb.stanford.edu
www.gsb.stanford.edu/ces

University of California, Irvine
Center for Entrepreneurship
  and Innovation
Graduate School of Management
Irvine, CA 92697
949-824-7311
www.uci.edu

University of California, San Diego
The Beyster Institute
The Rady School
La Jolla, CA 92093
858-826-1690
info@beysterinstitute.org
www.beysterinstitute.org

University of San Francisco
Gellert Foundation Family Business
  Center
School of Business and Management
2130 Fulton St.
San Francisco, CA 94117
415-422-5380
fbc@usfca.edu
www.usfca.edu/fbrc

University of the Pacific
Center for Entrepreneurship
Eberhardt School of Business
Stockton, CA 95211
209-946-2344
http://www1.pacific.edu/esb/
  entrecenters.html

University of California, Berkeley
Lester Center for Entrepreneurship
  and Innovation
Haas School of Business
510-642-4255
entrepreneurship@berkeley.edu
www.berkeley.edu

University of California,
  Los Angeles
Harold Price Center for
  Entrepreneurial Studies
John E. Anderson Graduate
  School of Management
Los Angeles, CA 90095
310-825-2985
esctr@anderson.ucla.edu
www.anderson.ucla.edu

University of San Diego
Leadership Institute for
  Entrepreneurship
School of Business Administration
598 Alcala Park
619-260-4186
life@sandiego.edu
http://life.sandiego.edu

University of Southern California
Greif Entrepreneurship Center
Center for Technology
  Commercialization
Bridge One Hall
Los Angeles, CA 90089
213-740-2976
kellen@marshall.usc.edu
www.usc.edu/org/techalliance

University of the Pacific
Institute for Family Business
Eberhardt School of Business
Stockton, CA 95211
888-439-2867
www.uop.edu

Pepperdine University
Center for Entrepreneurship
   and Technology Law
School of Law
Malibu, CA 90263
310-506-4000
ceti-info@law.pepperdine.edu
http://law.pepperdine.edu

California Polytechnic State
   University, Pomona
E-Business Department
College of Business Administration
Pomona, CA 91768
909-869-2383
www.csupomona.edu

Colorado

Adams State College
Small Business Development Center
School of Business, Room 115
208 Edgemont St.
Alamosa, CO 81102
719-587-7372
ascsbdc@adams.edu
www.adams.edu

Community College of Denver
Small Business Development Center
1445 Market St.
Denver, CO 80202
303-620-8076
denver.sbdc@den-chamber.org
http://ccd.rightchoice.org

Fort Lewis College
Small Business Development Center
1000 Rim Dr., 140 EBB
Durango, CO 81301
970-247-7009
www.fortlewis.edu

Front Range Community College
Small Business Development Center
125 South Howes St., Suite 150
Fort Collins, CO 80521
970-498-9295
sbdc@frii.com
www.frcc.cccoes.edu

Otero Community College
Small Business Development Center
1802 College Ave.
La Junta, CO
719-384-6959
sbdc@ojc.edu
www.ojc.edu

Pueblo Community College
Small Business Development Center
900 W. Orman Ave.
Pueblo, CO 81004
719-549-3224
www.pueblocc.edu

University of Colorado, Boulder
Entrepreneurship Center for Music
IMIG 18th and Euclid 301 UCB
303-492-6352
www.colorado.edu

University of Colorado, Colorado
   Springs
Small Business Development Center
1420 Auston Bluffs Pkwy.
719-272-7232
www.uccs.edu

University of Colorado, Denver
Bard Center for Entrepreneurship
535 16th Street, Suite 300
College of Business
303-620-4050
http://thunder1.cudenver.
   edu/bard

University of Northern Colorado
The Institute for Entrepreneurship
Kenneth W. Monfort
970-351-2764
monfortcollege@unco.edu
www.unco.edu

Connecticut

Central Connecticut State
   University
Entrepreneurship Program
School of Business
1615 Stanley St.
New Britain, CT 06050-4010
860-832-3205
www.ccsu.edu

Quinnipiac University
The Entrepreneurship Institute
School of Business
Hamden, CT 06518
203-582-8200
www.quinnipiac.edu

University Of Connecticut
Small Business Development Center
2100 Hillside Rd.
Storrs, CT 06269
860-486-4135
CSBDCInformation@business.
   uconn.edu
www.uconn.edu

University of Hartford
Entrepreneurial Studies
Barney School of Management
West Hartford, CT 06117
860-768-4100
www.hartford.edu

Other UConn SBDC locations:
Bridgeport 203-330-4813
   bridgeportCSBDC@business.
   uconn.edu
Danbury 203-743-556
   danburyCSBDC@business.
   uconn.edu
Groton 860-405-9002
   CgrotonCSBDC@business.
   uconn.edu

New Haven 203-782-4390
   newhavenCSBDC@business.
   uconn.edu
Stamford 203-359-3220
   stamfordCSBDC@business.
   uconn.edu
Waterbury 203-236-9983
   waterburyCSBDC@business.
   uconn.edu

Delaware

University of Delaware
Center for Economic Education
    and Entrepreneurship
102 Alfred Lerner Hall
Newark, DE 19716
302-831-2554
www.udel.edu/ceee

University of Delaware
Entrepreneurial Studies
102 MBNA—America Hall
Newark, DE 19716
302-831-6832
www.lerner.udel.edu

Delaware Technical and
    Community College
Small Business Development Center
103 West Price St.
Georgetown, DE 19947
302-856-1555
www.dtcc.edu

University of Delaware
Small Business Development Center
Delaware Technology Park
One Innovation Way, Suite 301
Newark, DE 19711
302-831-1555
www.udel.edu

University of Delaware, Wilmington
Small Business Development Center
1318 North Market St.
Wilmington, DE 19801
302-571-1555
www.udel.edu

District of Columbia

The George Washington University
Council for Family Enterprise
710 21st St., Suite 206
Washington, DC 20052
202-994-6380
www.gwu.edu

Southeastern University
Center for Entrepreneurship
501 I Street SW
Washington, DC 20024
202-478-8216
www.seu.edu

Florida

Florida Atlantic University
Small Business Development Center
Boca Raton, FL 33431
www.fausbdc.com

Florida Gulf Coast University
Institute for Entrepreneurship
Center for Leadership and
    Innovation
Fort Myers, FL 33965
239-590-7389
www.fgcu.edu/ife

Florida Gulf Coast University
Small Business Development Center
12751 Westlinks
Fort Myers, FL 33965
239-225-4220
http://cli.fgcu.edu/sbdc

Florida International University
Eugene Pino and Family Global
   Entrepreneurship Center
Ryder Building
Miami, FL 33199
305-348-1020
entrepreneurship@fiu.edu
www.entrepreneurship.fiu.edu

Nova Southeastern University
W. Wayne Huizenga School of
   Business and Entrepreneurship
3301 College Ave.
Fort Lauderdale, FL 33314
954-262-5000
infor@huizenga.nova.edu
www.huizenga.nova.edu

Stetson University
Prince Entrepreneurship Program
School of Business Administration
DeLand, FL 32723
386-822-7425
www.stetson.edu

University of Florida
Center for Entrepreneurship
   and Innovation
Warrington College of Business
Gainesville, FL 32611
352-273-0330
cei@cba.ufl.edu
www.ufventure.com

Florida Institute of Technology
Florida Tech Start
Melbourne, FL 32901
321-674-TECH
flstart@fit.edu
www.fit.edu/floridatechstart

Florida State University
The Jim Moran Institute for
   Global Entrepreneurship
College of Business
Tallahassee, FL 32306
850-644-3372
800-821-7515
www.fsu.edu

Rollins College
Entrepreneurship Center
Crummer Graduate School
   of Business
1000 Holt Ave.
Winter Park, FL 32789
407-691-1125
www.rollins.edu/
   entrepreneurship

University of Central Florida
Small Business Development Center
College of Business Administration
Orlando, FL 32816
407-420-4850
www.bus.ucf.edu/sbdc

University of North Florida
Small Business Development Center
Coggin School of Business
12000 Alumni Dr.
Jacksonville, FL 32224
904-620-2476
smalbiz@unf.edu
www.sbdc.unf.edu

University of South Florida
Center for Entrepreneurship
College of Business Administration
4202 E. Fowler Ave.
Tampa, FL 33620
813-974-1550
ce@coba.usf.edu
www.entrepreneurship.usf.edu

The University of Tampa
Florida Entrepreneurship and
    Family Business Program
Sykes College of Business
Tampa, FL 33606
813-253-3333, ext. 3782
http://ut.edu/institutes/cobcenters/
    fep/index.html

University of South Florida
Small Business Development Center
1101 Channelside Dr., Suite 210
Tampa, FL 33602
813-905-5817
www.sbdc.usf.edu

University of West Florida
Small Business Development Center
College of Business
Pensacola, FL 32514
850-473-7830
www.sbdc.uwf.edu

Georgia

Clark Atlantic University
Center for Entrepreneurship
School of Business Administration
223 James P. Brawly Dr.
Atlanta, GA 30314
404-880-8451
www.cau.edu

Clayton College
Small Business Development Center
P.O. Box 285
Morrow, GA 30260
770-961-3440
www.clayton.edu

Georgia Highlands
Small Business Development Center
415 E. 3rd St.
Rome, GA 30162
706-295-6326
www.highlands.edu

Clark Atlantic University
Small Business Development Center
School of Business Administration
223 James P. Brawly Dr.
Atlanta, GA 30314
404-880-8744
sbdc@cau.edu
www.sbdc.cau.edu

Emory University
Center for Entrepreneurship and
    Corporate Growth
Robert C. Goizueta Business School
1300 Clifton Rd.
Atlanta, GA 30322
404-727-4891
www.goizueta.emory.edu/cecg

Georgia Institute of Technology
Program for Engineering
    Entrepreneurship
Atlanta, GA 30332
404-894-2600
www.gatech.edu

Georgia Southwestern State
  University
Center for Business and
  Economic Development
School of Business Administration
Americus, GA 31709
229-931-2090
www.business.gsw.edu/busa/CBED

Georgia State University
Herman J. Russell Sr. International
  Center for Entrepreneurship
Robinson College of Business
Atlanta, GA 30303
404-651-2600
www.cba.gsu.edu/rec

Kennesaw State University
Small Business Development Center
Michael J. Coles College of Business
100 Chastain Rd., #0409
Kennesaw, GA 30144
770-423-6450
www.kennesaw.edu

State University of West Georgia
Center for New Business Ventures
Richards College of Business
Carrolton, GA 30118
770-838-3222
cnbv@westga.edu
www.westga.edu

University of Georgia
Selig Center for Economic Growth
Terry College of Business
Athens, GA 30602
706-425-2962
www.uga.edu

Georgia Southwestern State
  University
Small Business Development Center
800 Wheatley St.
Americus, GA 31709
229-931-2091
www.business.gsw.edu

Georgia State University
Small Business Development Center
Robinson College of Business
Atlanta, GA 30303
404-651-3550
sbdmbp@langate.gsu.edu
www.gsu.edu/sbdc

Reinhardt College
Small Business Development Center
McCamish School of Business
Waleska, GA 30183
770-720-5953
www.reinhardt.edu

State University of West Georgia
Small Business Development Center
Richards College of Business
Carrolton, GA 30118
678-839-5082
http://sbdc.westga.edu

University of Georgia
Small Business Development Center
Terry College of Business
Athens, GA 30602
706-542-7436
www.uga.edu

Valdosta State University
Small Business Development Center
Harlay Langdale Jr. College of
  Business Administration
Thaxton Hall, Room 100
Valdosta, GA 31698
229-245-3738
www.valdosta.edu

Guam

University of Guam
Pacific Islands Small Business
  Development Center
P.O. Box 5404
Mangilao, Guam 96923
671-735-2590
www.pacificsbdc.com

Hawaii

Chaminade University of Honolulu
Hogan Entrepreneurial Program
3140 Waialee Ave.
Honolulu, HI 96816
800-735-4711
www.chaminade.edu/academics/hogan

Hawaii Pacific University
Center for Business and the
  Community
College of Business Administration
Honolulu, HI 96813
808-544-0200
www.hpu.edu

University of Hawaii, Manoa
Pacific Asia Center for
  Entrepreneurship
College of Business Administration
Honolulu, HI 96822
808-956-5083
www.cba.hawaii.edu/pace

University of Hawaii, Manoa
Family Business Center of Hawaii
College of Business Administration
Honolulu, HI 96822
808-956-4298
www.uhm.hawaii.edu

University of Hawaii, Manoa
Pacific Business Center Program
2404 Maile Way
Honolulu, HI 96822
808-956-6286
pbcp@hawaii.edu
www.hawaii.edu/pbcp

University of Hawaii, Hilo
Small Business Development Center
100 Pauahi St., Suite 109
Hilo, HI 96720
808-933-0776
www.hawaii-sbdc.org

Idaho

Boise State University
Small Business Development Center
1910 University Dr.
Boise, ID
208-426-3875
www.boisestate.edu

College of Southern Idaho
Small Business Development Center
315 Falls Ave.
Evergreen Building, Room C77
Twin Falls, ID 83303
208-732-6450
http://www.csi.edu

Idaho State University
Small Business Development Center
1651 Alvin Ricker Dr.
Pocatello, ID 83209
208-232-4921
http://www.isu.edu

North Idaho College
Small Business Development Center
525 W. Clearwater Loop
Post Falls, ID 83854
208-666-8009
mmfaivre@nic.edu
www.nic.edu

Lewis-Clark State College
Small Business Development Center
500 8th Ave.
Lewiston, ID 83501
208-792-2465
www.lcsc.edu

Illinois

Bradley University
Turner Center for Entrepreneurship
Foster College of Business
141 Jobst Hall
Peoria, IL 61625
309-677-4321
www.bradley.edu/turnercenter

College of Dupage
Small Business Development Center
Glen Ellyn, IL 60137
630-942-2771
www.cod.edu/BPI/Sbdc.htm

Chicago State University
Small Business Development Center
9501 South King Dr.
Chicago, IL 60628
773-995-3938
www.csu.edu

College of Dupage
E-business Information Center
425 Fawell Blvd.
Glen Ellyn, IL 60137
630-942-2748
www.cod.edu

DePaul University
Coleman Entrepreneurship Center
College of Commerce
1 East Jackson Blvd.
Chicago, IL 60604
312-362-8625
cec@depaul.edu
www.coleman-center.org

Governors State University
Small Business Development Center
1 University Pkwy.
University Park, IL 60466
708-534-4929
www.govst.edu

Kaskaska College
Small Business Development Center
206 Main St.
Salem, IL 62881
618-548-9001
kcsbdc@kaskaska.edu
www.kc.cc.il.us/Business
   ServiceCenter

Loyola University Chicago
Family Business Center
Graduate School of Business
Chicago, IL 60611
312-915-6490
www.sba.luc.edu/centers/fbc

Northwestern University
Levy Institute for Entrepreneurial
   Practice
Kellogg School of Management
Evanston, IL 60208
847-491-4907
www.kellogg.northwestern.
   edu/academic/entrepreneurship

Eastern Illinois University
Business and Technology Institute
Lumpkin College of Business and
   Applied Sciences
Charleston, IL 61920
217-581-2913
www.eiu.edu/~bti

Illinois Institute of Technology
Ed Kaplan Entrepreneurial Studies
   Program
Chicago, IL 60616
312-567-3951
www.iit.edu/~entrepreneur

Illinois State University
Institute for Entrepreneurial Studies
College of Business
Normal, IL 61790
309-438-2994
www.cob.ilstu.edu/ies

Northwestern University
Heizen Center for Entrepreneurial
   Studies
Kellogg School of Management
Evanston, IL 60208
847-491-4907
www.kellogg.northwestern.edu/
   academic/entrepreneurship

Northwestern University
The Center for Family Enterprises
Kellogg School of Management
Evanston, IL 60208
847-491-5731
www.kellogg.northwestern.edu/
   academic/entrepreneurship

Rock Valley College
Rock River Valley Entrepreneurship
   Center
3301 N. Mulford Rd.
Rockford, IL 61114
815-921-2081
www.rockvalleycollege.edu

Southern Illinois University,
   Edwardsville
Small Business Development Center
200 University Park, Suite 1126
Edwardsville, IL 62026
618-650-2929
www.siue.edu

University of Chicago
Polsky Center for Entrepreneurship
Graduate School of Business
5807 South Woodlawn Ave.
Chicago, IL 60637
773-834-4525
polskycenter@ChicagoGSB.edu
www.uchicago.edu

University of Illinois, Urbana-
   Champaign
Small Business Development Center
1817 S. Neil St., Suite 201
Champaign, IL 61820
217-378-8535
uie-sbdc@extension.uiuc.edu
www.uiuc.edu

Southern Illinois University,
   Carbondale
Small Business Development Center
150 E. Pleasant Rd.
Carbondale, IL 62901
618-536-2424
sbdc@siu.edu
www.siuc.edu/~sbdc

Triton College
Small Business Development Center
200 Fifth Ave.
River Grove, IL 60171
708-456-0300, ext. 3593
www.triton.edu

University of Illinois, Chicago
Institute for Entrepreneurship
   Studies
College of Business Administration
601 S. Morgan
Chicago, IL 60607
312-996-2670
www.uic.edu

Western Illinois University
Small Business Development Center
Western Illinois Business and
   Technology Center
510 N. Pearl St.
Macomb, IL 61455
309-836-2640
www.wiusbdc.org

Indiana

Ball State University
Midwest Entrepreneurial Education
  Center
Miller College of Business
2000 W. University Ave.
Muncie, IN 47306
765-285-1560
www.bsu.edu/web/entrepreneurship

Indiana State University
Small Business Development Center
College of Business
Ninth and Sycamore
Terre Haute, IN 47809
812-237-7676
SBDC@indstate.edu
www.indstate.edu/schbus/sbdc

Indiana University-Purdue
  University, Fort Wayne
Business Resource Center
School of Business and Management
Fort Wayne, IN 46805
www.ipfw.edu/bms

Purdue University, Calumet
Entrepreneurship Center
School of Management
Hammond, IN 46323
219-989-2100
e-center@calumet.purdue.edu
www.calumet.purdue.edu

Huntington College
Entrepreneurship Program
Department of Business and
  Economics
Huntington, IN 46750
260-356-6000
www.huntington.edu

Indiana University
Johnson Center for
  Entrepreneurship and Innovation
Kelley School of Business
Bloomington, IN 47405
812-855-4248
jcei@indiana.edu
www.kelley.indiana.edu/jcei

Purdue University
Burton D. Morgan Center for
  Entrepreneurship
Discovery Park
Krannert Graduate School of
  Business
West Lafayette, IN 47907
765-494-6400
http://www.purdue.edu

University of Indianapolis
Center of Business Partnerships
School of Business
Indianapolis, IN 46227
800-232-8634
www.uindy.edu

University of Notre Dame
Gigot Center for Entrepreneurship
Mendoza College of Business
Norte Dame, IN 46556
574-631-3042
entrep.entrep1@nd.edu
www.nd.edu/~entrep

University of St. Francis
Family Business Center
Fort Wayne, IN 46808
260-434-7597
www.sf.edu/business

Iowa

Iowa State University
Pappajohn Center for
   Entrepreneurship
Ames, IA 50011
515-296-6532
www.isupjcenter.org

Iowa State University
Iowa Business Network
Ames, IA 50011
www.iabusnet.org

The University of Iowa
Pappajohn Entrepreneurial Center
108 John Pappajohn Business
   Building
Iowa City, IA 52242
319-335-1022
iowajpec@uiowa.edu
www.uiowa.edu

Drake University
Small Business Development Center
18601 Douglas Avenue
Urbandale, IA 50322
515-331-8954
www.iabusnet.org

Kansas

Benedictine College
Cray Center for Entrepreneurship
Atchison, KS 66002
913-360-7425
dhoy@benedictine.edu
www.benedictine.edu

Emporia State University
Small Business Development Center
Emporia, KS 66801
620-341-5308
SBDC@emporia.edu
www.emporia.edu

Fort Hays State College
Small Business Development Center
214 SW 6th Ave., Suite 301
Hays, KS 67601
785-296-6514
www.fhsu.edu/ksbdc

Pittsburg State University
Small Business Development Center
1501 S. Joplin
Pittsburg, KS 66762
620-235-4920
www.pittstate.edu

University of Kansas
Small Business Development Center
734 Vermont, Suite 104
Lawrence, KS 66045
785-843-8844
www.kusbdc.net

Wichita State University
Center for Entrepreneurship
1845 N. Fairmont
Wichita, KS 67260
316-978-3000
www.cfe.wichita.edu

Washburn University
Small Business Development Center
120 SE 6th St.
Topeka, KS 66621
785-234-3235
www.washburn.edu/sbdc

Wichita State University
Small Business Development Center
Metropolitan Complex
Wichita, KS 67260
316-978-3193
www.webs.wichita.edu/ksbdc

Kentucky

Eastern Kentucky University
Center for Economic Development,
    Entrepreneurship and Technology
521 Lancaster Ave.
Richmond, KY 40475
859-622-2334
www.cbt.eku.edu/cedet

Morehead State University
Small Business Development Center
College of Business
Morehead, KY 40351
606-783-2995
www.moreheadstate.edu

Northern Kentucky University
Fifth Third Bank Entrepreneurship
    Family Institute
Highland Heights, KY 41099
859-577-5931
www.53ei.org

Northern Kentucky University
Small Business Development Center
Highland Heights, KY 41099
859-577-5931
www.nku.edu/~sbdc

Eastern Kentucky University
Small Business Development Center
Richmond, KY 40475
1-877-358-7232
SBDC@centertech.com
www.sbdc.eku.edu

Murray State University
Small Business Development Center
Business Building So., Room 253
Murray, KY 42071
270-762-2856
www.murraystate.edu

Northern Kentucky University
Business Center
222 BEP Center
Highland Heights, KY 41099
859-572-6524
www.nku.edu/~fbc

Southeast Community College
Small Business Development Center
Middlesboro, KY 40965
606-242-2145, ext. 2021
www.SoutheastSBDC.com

University of Kentucky
Von Allmen Center for
 Entrepreneurship
Gatton College of Business
 and Economics
Lexington, KY 40506
859-257-3868
www.lexicc.com

Western Kentucky University
Small Business Development Center
2355 Nashville Rd.
Bowling Green, KY 42101
270-745-1905
www.wku.edu

Louisiana

Grambling State University
Young Entrepreneurs Program
Grambling, LA 71245
318-274-2346
yep.gsu@execs.com
www.gram.edu

Loyola University New Orleans
Small Business Development Center
New Orleans, LA 70118
504-864-7942
sbdc@loyno.edu
www.loyno.edu

University of Lousiville
Institute for Entrepreneurial
 Research
College of Business and Public
 Administration
Lousiville, KY 40292
502-852-4793
fiet@louisville.edu
www.cbpa.louisville.edu/fiet

Western Kentucky University
Center for Entrepreneurship
Gordon Ford College of Business
Bowling Green, KY 42101
270-745-6864
www.wku.edu/ec

Louisiana State University,
 Baton Rouge
Institute of Entrepreneurial
 Education and Family
 Business Studies
E.J. Ourso College of Business
 Administration
Baton Rouge, LA 70803
225-578-8778
busefbs@lsu.edu
www.bus.lsu.edu

McNeese State University
Small Business Development Center
Burton Business Center
Lake Charles, LA 70609
337-475-5529
www.mcneese.edu/colleges/bus/sbdc

Northwestern State University of
   Louisiana
Small Business Development Center
Natchitoches, LA 71497
318-357-5611
boyettd@nsula.edu
www.nsula.edu

Southeastern Louisiana University
Small Business Development Center
1514 Martens Dr.
Hammond, LA 70402
985-549-3831
sbdc@selu.edu
www.selu.edu/Academics/Business/
   SBDC

Southern University and
   Agricultural and Mechanical
   College
Small Business Development Center
College of Business
Baton Rouge, LA 70813
225-922-0998
www.subr.edu

Southern University, New Orleans
Small Business Development Center
College of Business
New Orleans, LA 70126
www.suno.edu

Tulane University
Levy-Rosenblum Institute for
   Entrepreneurship
A. B. Freeman School of Business
New Orleans, LA 70118
504-865-5400
www.tulane.edu

Tulane University
Family Business Center
A. B. Freeman School of Business
New Orleans, LA 70118
www.freeman.tulane.edu/fbc

University of Louisiana, Lafayette
Small Business Development Center
Lafayette, LA 70504
337-262-5345
www.louisiana.edu/Research/SBDC

University of Louisiana, Monroe
Entrepreneurship Study Center
College of Business
   Administration
Monroe, LA 71209
318-342-1100
www.nlu.edu

University of New Orleans
Small Business Development
   Center
New Orleans, LA 70148
504-539-9292
unossbdc@uno.edu
www.uno.edu

Xavier University
Entrepreneurial Center
New Orleans, LA 70125
513-745-3932
waymire@xu.edu
www.xavier.edu

Maine

University of Southern Maine
Center for Entrepreneurship
School of Business
68 High St.
Portland, ME 04104
207-780-5919
cesb@usm.maine.edu
www.usm.maine.edu/cesb

Maryland

Bowie State University
Institute for the Development of
    Entrepreneurship Achievement
14000 Jericho Park Rd.
Bowie, MD 20715
301-860-4000
www.bowiestate.edu

Frostburg State University
Small Business Development Center
College of Business
LaVale, MD 21502
301-729-2400
www.sbdc-wmd.com

Morgan State University
Center for Entrepreneurship
    and Strategy
Earl G. Graves School of
    Business and Management
Baltimore, MD 21251
443-885-3433
www.morgan-ces.org

College of Southern Maryland
Small Business Development Center
LaPlata, MD 20646
301-934-7583
www.sbdchelp.com

Loyola College in Maryland
The Center for Closely Held Firms
Joseph A. Sellinger School of
    Business and Management
Baltimore, MD 21210
410-617-2000
www.loyola.edu/chf

Morgan State University
Entrepreneurial Development
    and Assistance Center
Baltimore, MD 21251
443-885-3261
www.morgan.edu/academics/
    special/EDAC

Salisbury State University
Small Business Development Center
Salisbury, MD 21801
410-548-4419
sbdcuser@salisbury.edu
www.salisbury.edu/community/sbdc

University of Baltimore
Center for Technology
    Commercialization
Baltimore, MD 21201
410-837-4200
www.ubalt.edu

University of Maryland,
    College Park
Dingman Center for
    Entrepreneurship
Robert H. Smith School of Business
College Park, MD 20742
301-405-9545
www.rhsmith.umd.edu/dingman

University of Maryland,
    College Park
Maryland Technology Enterprise
    Institute
College Park, MD 20742
301-405-4105
www.erc.umd.edu

Massachusetts

Babson College
Arthur M. Blank Center for
    Entrepreneurship
Babson Park, MA 02457
781-239-4420
daniesq@babson.edu
http://www3.babson.edu/eship

Boston College
Business Institute
The Carroll School of Management
Chestnut Hill, MA 02467
617-552-0461
BCBI@bc.edu

Clark University
Small Business Development Center
Graduate School of Management
Worcester, MA 01610
508-793-7615
sbdc@clarku.edu
www.clarku.edu/offices/sbdc

Boston College
Small Business Management Center
The Carroll School of Management
Chestnut Hill, MA 02467
617-552-4091
sbdcmail@bc.edu
www.bc.edu/centers/sbdc

Boston University
Entrepreneurial Management
    Institute
School of Management
Boston, MA 02215
617-353-9391
www.bu.edu/entrepreneurship
www.bc.edu/schools/csom/bcbi

Harvard University
Arthur Rock Center for
    Entrepreneurship
Cambridge, MA 02138
617-495-6000
www.hbs.edu/entrepreneurship

Massachusetts Institute of Technology
Entrepreneurship Center
Cambridge, MA 02139
617-253-8653
ecenter@mit.edu
http://entrepreneurship.mit.edu

Salem State University
Small Business Development Center
Salem, MA 01970
978-542-6343
www.salemsbdc.org

Tufts University
Entrepreneurial Leadership Program
The Gordon Institute
Medford, MA 02155
617-627-3117
http://gordon.tufts.edu/
   leadership.htm

University of Massachusetts, Boston
Small Business Development Center
College of Management
Boston, MA 02125
617-287-7750
www.sbdc.umb.edu

University of Massachusetts,
   Dartmouth
Small Business Development Center
Charlton College of Business
North Dartmouth, MA 02747
508-673-9783
www.msbdc.org/semass

Worcester Polytechnic Institute
Collaborative for Entrepreneurship
Worcester, MA 01609
508-831-5761
www.wpi.edu

Northeastern University
Center for Family Business
College of Business Administration
Boston, MA 02115
617-373-7031
www.neu.edu

Suffolk University
Entrepreneurship Studies
Sawyer School of Management
Boston, MA 02108
617-573-8000

University of Massachusetts,
   Amherst
Small Business Development Center
Springfield, MA 01105
413-737-6712
www.msbdc.org

University of Massachusetts, Boston
Environmental Business and
   Technology Center
Boston, MA 02125
617-287-7723
www.ebtc.umb.edu

University of Massachusetts,
   Dartmouth
Center for Business Research
Charlton College of Business
North Dartmouth, MA 02747
508-989-8446
www.umassd.edu/cbr

Worcester State University
Center for Business and Industry
Worcester, MA 01602
508-929-8126
www.worcester.edu

Michigan

Central Michigan University
LaBelle Entrpreneurial Center
College of Business Administration
Mount Pleasant, MI 48859
989-774-4000
www.cba.cmich.edu/lec

Ferris State University
Small Business and
    Entrepreneurship Program
School of Management
Big Rapids, MI 49307
231-591-2427
www.ferris.edu

Grand Valley State College
Center for Entrepreneurship
Seidman School of Business
Allendale, MI 49401
616-331-7582
www.gvsu.edu/businesss/
    entrepreneurship ceit@oakland.edu

Oakland University
Center for Entrepreneurship
    in Information Technology
Rochester, MI 48309
248-370-3284
http://www2.oakland.edu/ceit

Saginaw Valley State University
Family Business Program
College of Business and
    Management
University Center, MI 48710
989-964-7497
www.svsu.edu/cbm

University of Michigan
Samuel Zell and Robert H. Lurie
    Institute for Entrepreneurial
    Studies
Ann Arbor, MI 48109
734-615-4419
zticontact@umich.edu
www.zli.bus.umich.edu

University of Michigan, Flint
Center for Entrepreneurship
    and Business Development
Flint, MI 48502
810-767-7373
www.umf-outreach.edu/business

Minnesota

Bethel College
School of Executive Leadership
St. Paul, MN 55112
651-638-6400
http://sel.bethel.edu

Metropolitan State University
Center for Women Entrepreneurs
    and Entrepreneurship Education
St. Paul, MN 55106
612-659-7259
women@entrepreneur.
    metrostate.edu
www.metrostate.edu/com/cwe

Minnesota State University,
  Moorhead
Small Business Development Center
Moorhead, MN 56563
218-477-2289
www.mnstate.edu/cbi/oldsite/
  SBDC.htm

University of Minnesota, Duluth
Small Business Development Center
Center for Economic Development
Duluth, MN 55812
218-726-7298
www.umdced.com

University of St. Thomas
John M. Morrison Center for
  Entrepreneurship
College of Business
St. Paul, MN 55105
651-962-4400
entrep@stthomas.edu
www.stthomas.edu

Mississippi

Alcorn State University
Center for Entrepreneurial Studies
School of Business
Alcorn State, MS 39096
601-877-3900
www.alcorn.edu/outreach/ces.htm

Delta State University
Small Business Development Center
College of Business
Cleveland, MS 38733
662-846-4236
dsusbdc@deltastate.edu
www.deltastate.edu

St. Cloud State University
The Harold Anderson
  Entrepreneurial Center
G. R. Herberger College of Business
St. Cloud, MN 56301
320-654-5420
www.stcloudstate.edu

University of Minnesota, Twin
  Cities
Center for Entrepreneurial Studies
Carlson School of Management
Minneapolis, MN 55455
612-625-2442
www.umn.edu/tc

Alcorn State University
Small Business Development Center
School of Business
Alcorn State, MS 39096
601-877-3901
www.alcorn.edu/outreach/sbdc.htm

Mississippi State University
Technology Resource Institute
Mississippi State, MS 39762
662-325-8122
trc@cobilan.msstate.edu
www.msstate.edu/dept/tri

Mississippi State University
Small Business Development Center
College of Business and Industry
Starksville, MS 39763
662-325-8684
sbdc@cobilan.msstate.edu
www.cbi.msstate.edu/cobi/sbdc

University of Mississippi
Small Business Development Center
School of Business Administration
Oxford, MS 38677
662-915-5001
msbdc@olemiss.edu
www.olemiss.edu/depts/mssbdc

University of Mississippi
Hearin Center for Enterprise
    Science
School of Business Administration
Oxford, MS 38677
662-915-7730
http://hces.bus.olemiss.edu

Missouri

Central Missouri State University
Institute for Entrepreneurial Studies
Harmon College of Business
    Administration
Warrensburg, MO 64093
660-543-4092
www.cmsu.edu

Central Missouri State University
Small Business Development Center
Harmon College of Business
    Adminstration
Warrensburg, MO 64093
660-543-4402
www.cmsu.edu/sbdc

Northwest Missouri State University
Small Business Development Center
Melvin and Valorie Booth College
    of Business and Professional
    Studies
Maryville, MO 64468
660-562-1701
www.nwmissouri.edu/sbdc

Saint Louis University
Jefferson Smurfit Center for
    Entrepreneurial Studies
John Cook School of Business
St. Louis, MO 63103
314-977-3850
jsces@slu.edu
business.slu.edu/centers/
    Jefferson_Smurfit

Truman State University
Small Business Development Center
Kirksville, MO 63501
660-785-4307
sbdc@truman.edu
http://sbdc.truman.edu

University of Missouri, Columbia
The Rural Entrepreneurship
 Initiative
College of Business
Columbia, MO 65211
573-882-2121
www.cpac.missouri.edu

University of Missouri, Kansas City
Entrepreneurial Growth Resource
 Center
Bloch School of Business and
 Public Administration
Kansas City, MO 64110
816-235-6075
egrc@umkc.edu
www.umkc.edu

University of Missouri, St. Louis
Center for Entrepreneurship
 and Economic Education
College of Business Administration
St. Louis, MO 63121
314-516-5000
www.umsl.edu/~econed

University of Missouri, Columbia
Small Business Development Center
College of Business
Columbia, MO 65211
573-882-7096
sbdc@missouri.edu
http://sbdc.missouri.edu

University of Missouri, Rolla
Center for Entrepreneurship and
 Outreach
1300 North Bishop
Rolla, MO 65409
573-341-4690
www.umrceo.net

Washington University in St. Louis
The Skandalaris Center for
 Entrepreneurial Studies
John M. Olin School of Business
314-935-4512
sep@olin.wustl.edu
www.olin.wustl.edu/acadRes/
 Entrepreneurship.cfm

Montana

Montana State University, Billings
Small Business Institute
College of Business
Billings, MT 59101
406-657-2295
www.msubillings.edu/cob

Montana State University, Bozeman
The Center for Entrepreneurship
 for the New West
College of Business
406-994-4423
info@centernewwest.com
www.montana.edu/cob/
 centernewwest

The University of Montana,Missoula
American Indian Business Leaders
School of Business Administration
Missoula, MT 59812
406-243-4879
www.umt.edu

Nebraska

Bellevue University
Entrepreneurship Leadership Center
Bellevue, NE 68005
402-293-2000
www.bellevue.edu

University of Nebraska, Omaha
Nebraska Business Development
   Center
College of Business Administration
Omaha, NE 68182
402-595-1158
http://nbdc.unomaha.edu

University of Nebraska, Kearny
Nebraska Business Development
   Center
Kearny, NE 68849
308-865-8344
www.unk.edu/acad/nbdc

University of Nebraska, Lincoln
Entrepreneurship Program
College of Business Administration
Lincoln, NE 68588
402-472-3353
entprenshp@unnotes.unl.edu
www.unl.edu

Nevada

Sierra Nevada College
Entrepreneurship Program
Department of Management
Incline Village, NV 89451
775-831-7799
www.sierranevada.edu

University of Nevada, Reno
Small Business Development Center
College of Business Administration
Reno, NV 89557
775-784-4912
nsbdc@unr.nevada.edu
www.unr.edu

University of Nevada, Las Vegas
Small Business Development Center
College of Business
Las Vegas, NV 89154
702-895-3362
nsbdc@unlv.nevada.com
www.unlv.edu

New Hampshire

Dartmouth College
Center for Private Equity and
   Entrepreneurship
Keene, NH 03435
Tuck School of Business
Hanover, NH 03755
603-646-0522
pecenter@dartmouth.edu
www.tuck.dartmouth.edu

Plymouth State University
Small Business Institute
Plymouth, NH 03264
603-535-2921
www.plymouth.edu/busdept/sbi

Rivier College
Small Business Development Center
Nashua, NH 03060
603-891-8884
www.nhsbdc.org/nashua.htm

University of New Hampshire
William Rosenberg International
   Center of Franchising
Whittemore School of Business
Durham, NH 03824
603-862-6455
http://wsbe.unh.edu

Keene State College
Small Business Development Center
603-358-2602
www.nhsbdc.org/keene.htm

Plymouth State University
Small Business DevelopmentCenter
Plymouth, NH 03264
603-535-2523
www.nhsbdc.org/plymouth.htm

University of New Hampshire
The Center for Venture Research
Whittemore School of Business
Durham, NH 03824
cvr@unh.edu
http://wsbe.unh.edu/cvr

University of New Hampshire
International Private Enterprise
   Center
Whittemore School of Business
Durham, NH 03824
cvr@unh.edu
http://wsbe.unh.edu

New Jersey

Fairleigh Dichinson University
Rothman Institute of
   Entrepreneurial Studies
Samuel J. Silberman College of
   Business Administration
Madison, NJ 07940
973-443-8842
rothman@fdu.edu
www.fdu.edu

Kean University
Gateway Institute
College of Business and Public
   Administration
Union, NJ 07083
908-629-7269
gateway@kean.edu
www.kean.edu/~gateway

New Jersey City University
Small Business Development Center
Jersey City, NJ 07305
201-200-2156
www.njsbdc.com

Rutgers, The State University of
    New Jersey
Center for Entrepreneurship
1111 Washington
Newark, NJ 07102
973-353-1062
http://entcent.rutgers.edu

Seton Hall University
Center for Entrepreneurial Studies
Stillman School of Business
South Orange, NJ 07079
973-275-2251
http://business.shu.edu/ces

Rider University
Small Business Institute
Lawrenceville, NJ 08648
609-896-5000
www.rider.edu/~sbi

Rutgers, The State University
    of New Jersey
Small Business DevelopmentCenter
49 Bleeker St.
Newark, NJ 07102
973-353-1927
www.njsbdc.com

William Patterson University
Small Business Development Center
College of Business
Trenton, NJ 08608
973-754-8695
www.wpunj.edu/COB

New Mexico

New Mexico State University
Center for Entrepreneurship
College of Business Administration
    And Economics
Las Cruces, NM 88003-8001
505-646-2470
http://cbae.nmsu.edu

New Mexico State University,
    Carlsbad
Small Business Development Center
Carlsbad, NM 88220
505-885-9531
www.nmsbdc.org/carlsbad

New Mexico State University,
    Alamogordo
Small Business Development Center
Alamogordo, NM 88310
505-434-5272
www.nmsbdc.org/alamogordo

New Mexico State University,
    San Juan College
Small Business Development Center
Farmington, NM 87402
505-566-3528
www.nmsbdc.org/farmington

University of New Mexico,
   Albuquerque
Program for Creative Enterprise
Robert O. Anderson Graduate
   School of Management
Albuquerque, NM 87131
505-277-3468
www.unm.edu

University of New Mexico, Gallup
Small Business Development Center
Gallup, NM 87301
505-863-6006
www.nmsbdc.org/gallup

New York

Alfred University
The Center for Family Business
Alfred, NY 14802
607-871-2111
http://business.alfred.edu/cfb.html

Boricua College
Small Business Development Center
Brooklyn, NY 11206
718-963-4112
www.nyssbdc.org

Bernard M. Baruch College of the
   City University of New York
Field Center for Entrepreneurship
Zicklin School of Business
New York, NY 10010
646-312-4790
FieldCenter@baruch.cuny.edu
www.baruch.cuny.edu

Buffalo State College, SUNY
Small Business Development Center
Buffalo, NY 14222
716-878-4030
buffalosbdc@yahoo.com
www.buffalostate.edu/
   facscenters.xml

Clarkson University
Shipley Center for Leadership
   and Entrepreneurship
School of Business
Potsdam, NY 13699
315-268-3811
shipley@clarkson.edu
www.clarkson.edu/business/shipley

College of Staten Island of the
   City University of New York
Small Business Development Center
Staten Island, NY 10314
718-982-2560
www.nyssbdc.org

Columbia University
The Eugene M. Lang Center for
   Entrepreneurship
Graduate School of Business
New York, NY 10027
212-854-3244
entprog@columbia.edu
http://www0.gsb.columbia.edu/
   entrepreneurship

SUNY Farmingdale
Small Business Development Center
Farmingdale, NY 11735
631-420-2765
www.nyssbdc.org

Cornell University
Center for Technology, Enterprise,
  and Commercialization
Ithaca, NY 14853
607-257-1081
www.cctec.cornell.edu

Lehamn College of the City
  University of New York
Small Business Development Center
Bronx, NY 10468
718-960-8806
www.nyssbdc.org

Mercy College
Small Business Development Center
Dobbs Ferry, NY 10522
914-375-2107
www.nyssbdc.org

Niagara University
Family Business Center
College of Business
Niagara Falls, NY 14109
716-286-8172
CBAcenters@niagara.edu
www.niagara.edu/business

Rensselear Polytechnic Institute
Severino Center for Technological
  Entrepreneurship
Lally School of Management
  and Technology
Troy, NY 12180
518-276-8398
www.rpi.edu

Hofstra University
Center for Entrepreneurship
  Development
Scott Skodnik Business
  Development Center
Hempstead, NY 11549
516-463-5285
www.hofstra.edu/com/bdc

Marist College
The Hudson River Valley Institute
Poughkeepsie, NY 12601
845-575-3052
hrvi@Marist.edu
www.hudsonrivervalley.net

New York University
Berkeley Center for Entrepreneurial
  Studies
Leonard N. Stern School of
  Business
New York, NY 10012
212-998-0070
www.nyu.edu

Pace University
Small Business Development Center
Lubin School of Business
New York, NY 10038
212-618-6655
SBDC@pace.edu
www.pace.edu

SUNY, Albany
Small Business Development Center
Albany, NY 12222
518-453-9567
www.albany.edu

SUNY, Buffalo
Technology Entrepreneurship
  Program
Buffalo, N 14260
716-645-2633
www.mgt.buffalo.edu

Syracuse University
Michael J. Falcone Center
  for Entrepreneurship
Department of Entrepreneurship
  and Emerging Enterprises
Martin J. Whitman School of
  Management
Syracuse, NY 13244
315-443-3445
www.som.syr.edu/eee/falcone

North Carolina

Appalachian State University
Watauga Entrepreneur
  Development Partnership
Appalachian Regional Development
  Institute
Walker College of Business
Boone, NC 28608
828-262-6161
www.ardi.appstate.edu

North Carolina State University
Entrepreneurship Education
  Initiative
College of Management
Raleigh, NC 27695
919-515-2011
http://entrepreneurship.ncsu.edu

UNC, Chapel Hill
Kenan Institute of Private
  Enterprise
Chapel Hill, NC 27599
919-962-8301
www.kenan-flagler.unc.edu/KI

Duke University
Center for the Advancement of
  Social Entrepreneurship
Fuqua School of Business
Durham, NC 27708
919-660-7823
case@fuqua.duke.edu
www.fuqua.duke.edu/centers/case

Queens University of Charlotte
Entrepreneurial Leadership Circle
McColl Graduate School of
  Business
Charlotte, NC 28274
704-337-2200
http://mccoll.queens.edu/elc

UNC, Charlotte
Rural Economic Development
  Center
Charlotte, NC 28223
704-358-3135
www.uncc.edu

The University of North
  Carolina, Wilmington
Small Business and Technology
  Development Center
School of Business
Wilmington, NC 28403
910-962-3744
www.csb.uncw.edu/sbtdc/index.htm

Wake Forest University
Angell Center for Entrepreneurship
Babcock Graduate School of
  Management
Winston-Salem, NC 27109
336-758-3689
www.mba.wfu.edu/ace

North Dakota

University of North Dakota
Small Business Development Center
College of Business and Public
  Administration
Grand Forks, ND 58202
www.ndsbdc.org

Ohio

Baldwin-Wallace College
Entrepreneurship Program
Division of Business Administration
Berea, OH 44017
440-826-2900
www.bw.edu/academics/bus/
  programs/entre

Bowling Green State University
Entrepreneurship Center
Bowling Green, OH 43403
419-372-2581
www.cba.bgsu.edu

Case Western Reserve   University
Entrepreneurship Division
Weatherhead School of
  Management
Cleveland, OH 44106
216-368-2076
www.weatherhead.case.edu

John Carroll University
The Edward M. Muldoon Center
  for Entrepreneurship
University Heights, OH 44118
216-397-1886
www.jcu.edu

Kent State University
The Entrepreneurial Academy
Graduate School of Management
Kent, OH 44242
216-541-4140
http://imagine.kent.edu/staff/centers

The Ohio State University
Center for Entrepreneurship
Max M. Fisher College of Business
Columbus, OH 43210
614-292-4085
www.centerforentrepreneurship.com

The University of Akron
Fitzgerald Institute for
    Entrepreneurial Studies
College of Business Administration
Akron, OH 44325
330-972-8479
www.uakron.edu

University of Dayton
Crotty Center for Entrepreneurial
    Leadership
School of Business Administration
Dayton, OH 45469
937-229-3127
www.sba.udayton.edu/entrepreneur

University of Toledo
Small Business and Entrepreneurship
    Institute
College of Business Administration
Toledo, OH 43606
419-530-2087
http://sbei.utoledo.edu

Miami University
Thomas C. Page Center for
    Entrepreneurship
Richard T. Farmer School of
    Business Administration
Oxford, OH 45056
513-529-1221
www.sba.muohio.edu/
    pagecenter/pagecenternew

Ohio University
Small Business Development Center
Athens, OH 45701
www.odod.state.oh.us/edd/osb/sbdc

University of Cincinnati
Enterprise@UC
College of Business
Cincinnati, OH 45221
513-556-7144
enterprise@uc.edu
www.business.uc.edu/enterprise

University of Toledo
Center for Family Business
College of Business Administration
Toledo, OH 43606
419-530-4058
www.utoledo.edu

Wright State University
Small Business Development Center
Raj Soin College of Business
Dayton, OH 45435
937-775-3503
www.wright.edu

Xavier University
Entrepreneurial Center
Williams College of Business
Cincinnati, OH 45207
745-513-2927
www.xu.edu

Youngstown State University
The Nathan and Francis Monus
　Entrepreneurship Center
Warren P. Williamson Jr. College
　of Business Administration
Youngstown, OH 44555
www.wcba.ysu.edu/nathan.htm

Oklahoma

East Central University
Small Business Development Center
Ada, OK 74820
580-436-3190
www.ecok.edu

Northwestern Oklahoma State
　University
Small Business Development Center
Alva, OK 73717
580-327-8610
www.nwosu.edu/osbdc

Oklahoma State University
Center for Entrepreneurship and
　Economic Development
Spears School of Business
Stillwater, OK 74078
spears-infor@okstate.edu
http://spears.okstate.edu

Rose State College
Small Business Development Center
Midwest City, OK 73110
405-733-7348
www.rose.edu

Southwestern Oklahoma State
　University
Small Business Development Center
Weatherford, OK 73096
580-774-7096
www.swosu.edu/cebd

University of Central Oklahoma
Small Business Development Center
Edmond, OK 73034
www.oklahomasmallbusiness.org

University of Oklahoma
Michael F. Price Entrepreneurship
　Center
Norman, OK 73019
405-325-3611
http://price.ou.edu/entrep

Oregon

University of Oregon
Center for Law and Entrepreneurship
School of Law
Eugene, OR 97403
541-346-3852
www.law.uoregon.edu/org/cle

Portland State University
Interdisciplinary Center for Law
  and Entrepreneurship
Portland, OR 97207
503-725-3757
www.pdx.edu

University of Portland
Center for Entrepreneurship
Portland, OR 97203
503-943-7782
www.up.edu

Oregon State University
Austin Entrepreneurship Program
College of Business
Corvallis, OR 97331
541-737-2551
www.bus.oregonstate.edu/programs/
  austin_entrep.htm

Southern Oregon University
Small Business Development Center
Ashland, OR 97520
www.bizcenter.org/medford

University of Oregon
Lundquist Center for
  Entrepreneurship
Charles H. Lundquist College of
  Business
Eugene, OR 97403
541-346-3420
http://lcb.uoregon.edu/lce

Pennsylvania

Bucknell University
Small Business Development Center
Lewisburg, PA 17837
570-577-1249
www.bucknell.edu/sbdc

Clarion University
Small Business Development Center
Clarion, PA 16214
814-393-2060
www.clarion.edu/sbdc

Carnegie Mellon University
The Donald H. Jones Center for
  Entrepreneurship
Pittsburgh, PA 15213
412-268-5382
emerson@andrew.cmu.edu
www.cmu.edu

Drexel University
Laurance A. Baida Center for
  Entrepreneurship in Technology
Bennett S. LeBow College of
  Business
Philadelphia, PA 19104
215-895-0301
www.lebow.drexel.edu/baiada/
  baiada.html

Duquesne University
Chrysler Small Business
  Development Center
Pittsburgh, PA 15282
412-396-6233
duqsbdc@duq.edu
www.duq.edu

Grove City College
Entrepreneurship Program
100 Campus Dr.
Grove City, PA 16127
724-458-2000
entrepreneurship@gcc.edu
www.gcc.edu

Kutztown University
Small Business Development Center
Kutztown, PA 717-232-3270
www.kutztownsbdc.org

Lehigh University
Small Business Development Center
College of Business and Economics
Bethlehem, PA 18015
610-758-5205
insbdc@lehigh.edu
http://www.lehigh.edu

Penn State University
Farrell Center for Corporate
  Innovation and Entrepreneurship
Smeal College of Business
State College, PA 16802
814-865-4593
www.smeal.psu.edu/fcfe

Gannon University
Small Business Development Center
Erie, PA 16541
814-871-7232
www.gannon.edu

Indiana University of Pennsylvania
Small Business Development Center
Indiana, PA 15705
724-357-7915
www.eberly.iup.edu/sbitemp/
  sbdc.htm

Lehigh University
Musser Center for Entrepreneurship
College of Business and Economics
Bethlehem, PA 18015
610-758-3980
www.lehigh.edu/~incbeug/centers/
  musser_center.html

Lock Haven University
Small Business Development Center
Lock Haven, PA 17745
570-893-2589
www.lhup.edu/sbdc/

Robert Morris University
Massey Center for Business
  Innovation and Development
Moon Township, PA 15108
412-227-6842
mcbid@rmu.edu
www.robert-morris.edu

St. Vincent College
Small Business Development Center
Latrobe, PA 15650
724-537-4572
www.sbdc.stvincent.edu

University of Pennsylvania
Sol. C. Snider Entrepreneurial
    Research Center
The Wharton School
Philadelphia, PA 19104
215-898-4861
www.upenn.edu

University of Pennsylvania
    Small Business Clinic
Penn Law
Philadelphia, PA 19104
215-898-8044
www.law.upenn.edu/clinic/sbc

Wilkes University
Allan P. Kirby Center for Free
    Enterprise and Entrepreneurshi
Wilkes-Barre, PA 18766
800-945-5378
www.wilkes.edu

Rhode Island

Bryant College
Small Business Development Center
Smithfield, RI 02917
401-232-6111
www.risbdc.org

Temple University
The Innovation and
    Entrepreneurship Institute
Fox School of Business and
    Management
Philadelphia, PA 19122
215-204-3080
iei@temple.edu
www.temple.edu

University of Pittsburgh
Institute for Entrepreneurial
    Excellence
Joseph M. Katz Graduate School
    of Business
Pittsburgh, PA 15260
412-648-1544
www.pitt.edu

University of Scranton
Small Business Development Center
Scranton, PA 18510
570-941-7588
http://sbdc.scranton.edu

Johnson and Wales University
The Larry Friedman International
    Center for Entrepreneurship
College of Business
Providence, RI 02903
401-598-1000
www.jwu.edu

South Carolina

Clemson University
Arthur M. Spiro Center for
　Entrepreneurial Leadership
College of Business
Clemson, SC 29634
864-656-7235
spiro@clemson.edu
http://business.clemson.edu/Spiro

Clemson University
Small Business Development Center
Charleston, SC 29423
864-656-3227
http://business.clemson.edu/SBDC

College of Charleston
Tate Center for Entrepreneurship
Consortium for Liberal Education
　and Entrepreneurship
Charleston, SC 29424
843-953-5501
www.cofc.edu/entrepreneur
　consortium

University of South Carolina
Faber Entrepreneurship Center
Darla Moore School of
　and Business
Columbia, SC 29208
803-777-5961
http://dmsweb.moore.sc.edu/faber

Winthrop University
Entrepreneurship Program
College of Business Administration
Rock Hill, SC 29733
803-323-2186
http://cba.winthrop.edu

South Dakota

Black Hills State University
Center for Business and
　Entrepreneurship
Spearfish, SD 57799
605-642-6091
www.bhsu.edu/businesstechnology/cbe

South Dakota State University
Entrepreneurship Program
Brookings, SD 57007
605-688-6522
www.sdstate.edu

University of Sioux Falls
Center for Women Business Institute
Sioux Falls, SD 57105
605-331-6697 605-677-5287
www.usiouxfalls.edu/
　professionalstudies/
cfw/business/cfw_business.htm

The University of South Dakota
Small Business Development Center
Vermillion, SD 57069
www.usd.edu/sbdc

Tennessee

Austin Peay State University
Small Business Development Center
Clarksville, TN 37044
931-221-7816
www.apsu.edu

East Tennessee State University
Small Business Development Center
College of Business
Johnson City, TN 37614
423-439-8505
www.etsu.edu

Middle Tennessee State University
Entrepreneurial Studies
College of Business
Murfreesboro, TN 37132
615-898-2902
entre@mtsu.edu
www.mtsu.edu

Middle Tennessee State University
Small Business Development Center
501 Memorial Blvd.
Murfreesboro, TN 37132
615-898-2745
www.mtsu.edu

Southern Adventist University
Entrepreneurship Program
School of Business and Management
Collegedale, TN 37315
423-236-2751
http://business.southern.edu

Tennessee State University
Small Business Development Center
College of Business
Nashville, TN 37209
615-963-7179
http://sbdc.logicmediagroup.com

Tennessee Technological University
Center for Small Business Consulting
College of Business Administration
Cookeville, TN 38505
931-372-6116
cbc@tntech.edu
www.tntech.edu/cob/cbc.htm

Tennessee Technological University
Small Business Development Center
College of Business Administration
Cookeville, TN 38505
931-372-3648
www.tntech.edu/sbdc

The University of Tennessee,
   Knoxville
James L. Clayton Center for
   Entrepreneurial Law
Knoxville, TN 37996
865-974-9917
www.law.utk.edu

Vanderbilt University
Owen Entrepreneurship Center
Owen Graduate School of
   Management
Nashville, TN 37240
615-322-2534
oec@owen.vanderbilt.edu
http://www2.owen.vanderbilt.
   edu/oec

Texas

Angelo State University
Small Business Development Center
College of Business
San Angelo, TX 76909
325-942-2098
SBDC@angelo.edu
www.acu.edu

Baylor University
Center for Entrepreneurship
Hankamer School of Business
Waco, TX 76798
254-710-2265
www.baylor.edu/business/
    entrepreneur

Houston Baptist University
Entrepreneurship Program
College of Business and Economics
Houston, TX 77074
281-649-3000
www.hbu.edu

Lamar University
Institute for Entrepreneurial Studies
College of Business
Beaumont, TX 77710
409-880-8888
www.lamar.edu

Kilgore College
Small Business Development Center
Longview, TX 75604
903-757-5857
www.kilgore.edu

Midwestern State University
Small Business Development Center
Wichita Falls, TX 76308
940-397-4373
www.msusbdc.org

North Central Texas College
Small Business Development Center
Gainesville, TX 76241
940-668-4220
www.nctc.edu

Rice University
Rice Alliance for Technology and
    Entrepreneurship
Jones Graduate School of
    Management
Houston, TX 77251
713-348-3443
alliance@rice.edu
www.alliance.rice.edu/alliance

St. Edward's University
TXEntre
Graduate School of Management
Austin, TX 78704
512-428-1287
txentre@acad.stedwards.edu
www.stedwards.edu

Sam Houston State University
Small Business Development Center
College of Business Administration
Huntsville, TX 77341
936-294-3737
http://sbdc.shsu.edu

Southern Methodist University
Caruth Institute for Entrepreneurship
Edwin L. Cox School of Business
Dallas, TX 75275
214-768-3689
caruth@mail.cox.smu.edu
www.cox.smu.edu

Texas A&M University
Center for New Ventures and
   Entrepreneurship
Mays Business School
College Station, TX 78041
979-845-8581
http://business.tamu.edu/cnve

Texas Southern University
Center for Entrepreneurship and
   Executive Development
Jesse H. Jones School of Business
Houston, TX 77004
713-313-7011
www.tsu.edu

Texas Tech University
Small Business Development Center
Lubbock, TX 79409
806-745-1637
www.ttusbdc.org/lubbock

Texas Tech University, Abilene
Small Business Development Center
Abilene, TX 79602
325-670-0300
www.ttusbdc.org/abilene

Tarleton State University
Small Business Development Center
Stephenville, TX 76402
254-968-9330
www.tsusbdc.org

Texas Christian University
The Ruffel Center for
   Entrepreneurial Studies
M. J. Neeley School of Business
Fort Worth, TX 76129
817-257-6544
www.tcu.edu

Texas State University, San Marcos
Small Business Development Center
College of Business Administration
San Marcos, TX 78666
512-225-9888
sbdc@business.txstate.edu
www.txstate.edu

Texas Tech University
Center for Entrepreneurial and
   Family Business
Jerry S. Rawls College of Business
Lubbock, TX 79409
806-742-2011
www.texastech.edu

University of Houston
Center for Entrepreneurship and
   Innovation
Bauer College of Business
Houston, TX 77204
713-743-4752
www.bauer.uh.edu/cei

University of Houston, Victoria
Small Business Development Center
Victoria, TX 77901
361-575-8944
sbdc@uhv.edu
www.sbdcvictoria.com

University of Texas, Austin
Herb Kelleher Center for
   Entrepreneurship
McCombs School of Business
Austin, TX 78712
512-471-5921
www.mccombs.utexas.edu/
research/hkcenter

University of Texas, San Antonio
Institute for Economic Development
College of Business
San Antonio, TX 78249
210-458-2020
ied@utsa.edu
www.utsa.edu

University of Texas, Permian Basin
Small Business Development Center
School of Business
Odessa, TX 79762
432-552-2455
www.utpb.edu

University of Houston
Small Business Development Center
Bauer College of Business
Huston, TX 77204
713-752-8444
www.sbdcnetwork.uh.edu

University of North Texas
Murphy Enterprise Center
College of Business Administration
Denton, TX 76203
940-565-2848
www.murphycenter.unt.edu

University of Texas, El Paso
Center for Hispanic
   Entrepreneurship
College of Business Administration
El Paso, TX 79968
915-747-5000
www.utep.edu

University of Texas, Pan American
Center for Entrepreneurship and
   Economic Development
College of Business Administration
956-81-3361
http://www.panam.edu

West Texas A&M University
Entrepreneurial Resource Network
T. Boone Pickens College of
   Business
Canyon, TX 79016
www.wtamu.edu

Utah

Brigham Young University
Center for Entrepreneurship
Marriott School of Management
Provo, UT 84602
801-422-5654
http://www.byu.edu

University of Utah
Lassonde New Venture
   Development Center
David Eccles School of Business
Salt Lake City, UT 84112
801-581-8504
www.utah.edu

Utah Valley State University
Entrepreneurship Program
School of Business
Orem, UT 84058
801-863-4636
www.uvsc.edu

Weber State University
Small Business Development Center
John B. Goddard School of Business
   and Economics
Ogden, UT 84408
801-626-7232
www.weber.edu

Weber State University
Williams H. Child Center for
   Entrepreneurship
John B. Goddard School of
   Business and Economics
Ogden, UT 84408
801-626-7476
www.weber.edu

Vermont

Lynden State College
Entrepreneurship Program
Business Administration
Lyndenville, VT 05851
802-626-6200
www.lsc.vsc.edu

University of Vermont
Vermont Family Business Initiative
School of Business Administration
Burlington, VT 05405
802-656-3175
business@bsad.uvm.edu
www.uvm.edu

Virginia

George Mason University
Center for Entrepreneurship
Department of Management
Fairfax, VA 22030
703-993-1880
www.gmu.edu

Hampton University
Center for Entrepreneurial Study
School of Business
Hampton, VA 23668
757-727-5361
www.hamptonu.edu

James Madison University
Center for Entrepreneurship
College of Business
Harrisonburg, VA 22807
540-568-3022
www.jmu.edu/cfe

University of Virginia
Center for Growth Enterprises
Darden Graduate School of Business
  Administration
Charlottesville, VA 22903
www.virginia.edu

University of Virginia
The Batten Institute
Darden Graduate School of Business
  Administration
Charlottesville, VA 22903
434-243-4300
www.darden.edu/batten

Virginia Polytechnic Institute and
  State University
Small Business Institute
Pamplin College of Business
Blacksburg, VA 24061
www.cob.vt.edu/cob/services

Washington

Eastern Washington University
Center for Entrepreneurial Activities
College of Business Administration
  and Public Administration
Cheney, WA 99004
509-358-2254
www.ewu.edu/x3606.xml

Pacific Lutheran University
Family Enterprise Institute
School of Business
Tacoma, WA 98447
253-535-7250
fament@plu.edu
www.plu.edu/~fament

Seattle University
Entrepreneurship Center
Albers School of Business and
Economics
Seattle, WA 98122
206-296-6000
www.seattleu.edu/asbe/ec

Gonzaga University
American Indian Entrepreneurship
School of Business Administration
Spokane, WA 99258
509-324-4622
chatman@jepsou.gonzaga.edu
www.gonzaga.edu

Pacific Lutheran University
E-commerce and Technology
  Management Center
School of Business
Tacoma, WA 98447
253-535-7252
eplu@plu.edu
http://eplu.plu.edu

University of Washington
Center for Technology
Business School
Seattle, WA 98195
206-685-9868
http://depts.washington.edu/cte

Washington State University
Center for Entrepreneurial Studies
College of Business and Economics
Pullman, WA 99164
entrepreneurship@cbe.wsu.edu
www.wsu.edu

Western Washington University
Small Business Development Center
College of Business and Economics
Bellingham, WA 98225
360-733-4014
www.cbe.wwu.edu/sbdc

West Virginia

West Virginia University
Entrepreneurship Center
College of Business and Economics
Morgantown, WV 26506
304-293-7221
www.be.wvu.edu/ec

Wisconsin

Marquette University
The Kohler Center for
   Entrepreneurship
College of Business Administration
Milwaukee, WI 53201
414-288-0670
www.mukohlercenter.org

University of Wisconsin, Eau Claire
Entrepreneur Program
College of Business
Eau Claire, WI 54702
715-736-5199
www.uwecep.com

University of Wisconsin, Green Bay
Small Business Development Center
Green Bay, WI 54311
920-496-2114
www.uwgb.edu/sbdc/

University of Wisconsin, La Crosse
Small Business Development Center
La Crosse, WI 54601
608-785-8782
www.uwlax.edu/sbdc

University of Wisconsin, Madison
Weinert Center for Entrepreneurship
School of Business
Madison, WI 53706
608-262-8640
www.wisc.edu

University of Wisconsin, Milwaukee
Bostrum Center for Business
   Competitiveness, Innovation,
   and Entrepreneurship
School of Business Administration
Milwaukee, WI 53201
414-229-6260
www.uwm.edu

University of Wisconsin, Oshkosh
Small Business Development Center
College of Business Administration
Oshkosh, WI 54901
800-232-8939
www.ccp.uwosh.edu

University of Wisconsin, Platteville
Small Business Development Center
Platteville, WI 53818
800-362-5515
www.uwplatt.edu/swsbdc

University of Wisconsin, Stevens
   Point
Small Business Development Center
Stevens Point, WI 54481
715-346-3838
www.uwsp.edu/extension/sbdc

University of Wisconsin, Whitewater
Small Business Development Center
Whitewater, WI 53190
262-472-3217
ask-sbdc@uww.edu
www.uww.edu/sbdc

University of Wisconsin, Parkside
Small Business Development Center
College of Business and Technology
Kenosha, WI 53141
262-898-7414
www.parksidesbdc.com

University of Wisconsin, River Falls
Small Business Development Center
River Falls, WI 54022
715-425-0620
sbdc@uwrf.edu
www.uwrf.edu/cbe/sbdc

University of Wisconsin, Superior
Small Business Development Center
Superior, WI 54880
715-394-8351
www.uwsuper.edu

Wyoming

University of Wyoming
Entrepreneurship
College of Business
Laramie, WY 82070
307-766-4194
www.uwyo.edu

Please Note: Besides those listed here, there are over a hundred other Small Business Development Offices scattered throughout America, sponsored by a local community college, chamber of commerce, or other nonprofit organization. You can find the one closest to you by logging on to www.asbdc-us.org.

Australia

Victoria University
Small Business Research Unit
Faculty of Business and Law
Melbourne, Victoria
www.business.vu.edu.au
61-3-9919-4000

Murdoch University
Entrepreneurship and Business
 Innovation Program
Murdoch School of Business
Perth, Western Australia
www.mbs.murdoch.edu.au

Curtin University of Technology
The BankWest Entrepreneurship
 and Business Development Unit
Curtin Business School
Perth, Western Australia
www.cbs.curtin.edu.au
ebduinfo@cbs.curtin.edu.au
61-8-9266-4555

RMIT University
RMIT Entrepreneurship Centre
RMIT Business School
Melbourne, Victoria
www.rmit.edu.au
61-13-9925-1383

University of South Australia
Centre for the Development of
 Entrepreneurship
Division of Business
Perth, South Australia
http://business.unisa.edu.au/cde
61-8-8302-0179

Gibaran Business School
Entrepreneurship Institute Australia
Adelaide, So. Australia
www.eia.sa.edu.au
gibaran@gibaran.edu.au
61-8-8212-8100

University of New South Wales
Entrepreneurship and Strategy
 Program
Australian Graduate School of
 Management
Sydney, N.S.W.
www2.agsm.edu.au
61-2-9931-9200

Canada

HEC Montreal
Le Centre d'entrepreneurship
Montreal, Quebec
www.hec.ca/entrepreneurship
514-340-5693

University of Alberta
Canadian Centre for Social
 Entrepreneurship
Edmonton, Alberta
www.bus.ualberta.ca/ccse
ccse@ualberta.ca
780-492-0187

St. Mary's University
Small Business & Entrepreneurship
   Program
Sobey School of Business
Halifax, Nova Scotia
www.stmarys.ca
902-496-8280

Royal Roads University
Entrepreneurial Management
   Program
School of Business
Victoria, B.C.
www.royalroads.ca
250-391-2511

University of Calgary
Centre for Family Business
   Management and
   Entrepreneurship
Haskayne School of Business
Calgary, Alberta
www.haskayne.ucalgary.ca
403-220-5685

McGill University
Dobson Centre for Entrepreneurial
Studies
Montreal, Quebec
www.dobsoncentre.mcgill.ca
514-398-4024

University of Waterloo
Centre for Business,
   Entrepreneurship and Technology
Waterloo, Ontario
http://cbet.uwaterloo.ca
519-888-4567 x 7167

University of Victoria
Entrepreneurship Program
Faculty of Business
Victoria, B.C.
www.business.uvic.ca
business@business.uvic.ca
250-721-6613

University of Manitoba
The Aspen Centre for
   Entrepreneurship
I.H. Aspen School of Business
Winnipeg, Manitoba
www.umanitoba.ca
www.umanitoba.ca

China

Fudan University
Entrepreneurship and Venture
   Capital Research Center
School of Management
Shanghai
www.fdms.fudan.edu.cn/en
6-564-2413

Fudan University
Business Development and
   Management Innovation Center
School of Management
Shanghai
www.fdms.fudan.edu.cn/en
6-564-2413

Cyprus

Cyprus International Institute of
    Management
Entrepreneurship and Innovation in
    Business Program/Family Business Program
Nicosia
www.ciim.ac.cy
357-2-246-2246

France

INSEAD
3i Venturelab
Fontainebleau Cedex
www.insead.edu/entrepreneurship
33-1-60-72-43-74

INSEAD
Wendel International Centre for
    Family Enterprise
Fontainebleau Cedex
www.insead.edu/facultyresearch/
    research/WICFE.htm
family-firms@insead.edu
33-1-60-72-92-50

EM Lyon
The Entrepreneurship Center
Lyon
www.em-lyon.com
entrepreneurs@em-lyon.com
33-4-78-33-79-54

ESSEC Business School
Venture Incubator
Cergy-Pontoise
www.essec.edu/essec-business-school
33-1-34-43-30-00

ENPC MBA
Technology and Innovation
    Management and
    Entrepreneurship Center
School of International
    Management
Paris
www.enpcmbaparis.com
33-1-44-58-28-52

Hong Kong

Lignan University
Hong Kong Institute of Business
    Studies
www.ln.edu.hk/hkibs
hkibs@ln.edu.hk
852-3400-2811

Hong Kong Polytechnic University
Institute for Enterprise
www.ife.polyu.edu.hk/index.asp
pdadmin@inet.polyu.edu.hk
852-3400-2811

University of Hong Kong
Chinese Management Center
School of Business
www.business.hku.hk/
   research.centres/cmc
cmcentre@hkusua.hku.hk
852-2547-6120

Ireland

University College
Innovation and Technology Centre
Dublin
www.ucd.ie
nova@ucd.ie
353-1-716-3707

Netherlands

Erasmus University
Center for Entrepreneurship
Rotterdam School of Management
Rotterdam
www.rsm.nl
31-10-408-2222

New Zealand

Massey University
Centre for Small and Medium
   Enterprises
Wellington
http://sme-centre.massey.ac.nz
64-4-801-5799

Korea

Konkuk University
Department of Small Business
   Studies
Seoul
www.konkuk.ac.kr/eng
02-450-3114

Norway

BI Norwegian School of
   Management
Innovation and Entrepreneurship
   Program
Sandvika
www.bi.no
infor@bi.no
47-67-55-7000

University of Aukland
Innovation and Entrepreneurship
   Program
Business School
Aukland
www.business.auckland.ac.nz
comenquiry@auckland.ac.nz
64-9-373-7599 ext, 87186

Philippines

University of San Carlos
Marketing and Entrepreneurship
  Program
College of Commerce
Cebu City
www.usc.edu.ph
63-32-253-1000

De La Salle University
Center for Business and Economics
  Research and Development
College of Business and Economics
Manilla
www.dlsu.edu.ph/research/centers/
  cberd
63-1-524-0489

University of Asia and the Pacific
Entrepreneurial Management
  Program
School of Management
Pasig City
www.uap.edu.ph

Asian Institute of Management
Asian Center for Entrepreneurship
Makati City
www.aim.edu.ph
ace_admissions@aim.edu.ph
63-2-892-4011 x 105

Saint Louis University
Institute for Small Scale Industries
  Foundation
Baguio City
www.slu.edu.ph/research/eissif.htm
63-74-442-3043

Singapore

INSEAD
International Center for
  Entrepreneurship
www.insead.edu/facultyresearch/
research/ICE.htm
linda.goh@insead.edu

National University of Singapore
Entrepreneurship Program
www.nus.edu.sg/nec
necquery@nus.edu.sg
65-6874-3018

South Africa

University of the Western Cape
Entrepreneurship Development Unit
Department of Management
Bellville
www.uwc.ac.za/academic
21-51-401-2874

University of the Free State
Centre for Business Dynamics
Faculty of Economics &
  Management
Bloemfontein
www.uovs.ac.za

University of Capetown
Centre for Innovation &
    Entrepreneurship
Graduate School of Business
Green Pointe
www.gsb.uct.ac.za
CIE@gsb.uct.ac.za
27-21-406-1470

Spain

Instituto de Empresa
Entrepreneurship Information Center
Madrid
www.ie.edu
Entrepreneurship@ie.edu
34-91-568-9600

ESADE Business School
Entrepreneurship Center
Barcelona
www.esade.edu
34-93-280-6162

University of Navarra
Center for Family-Owned Businesses
and Entrepreneurship
IESE Business School
Barcelona
www.iese.edu
34-93-253-4200

Taiwan

Chaoyang University of Technology
Business Incubation Center
College of Management
Wufong Township
www.cyut.edu.tw
mcollege@mail.cyut.edu.tw
886-4-232-3000

National Chiau-Tung University
Legal Center for Enterprise and
    Entrepreneurship
Hsinchu
www.nctu.edu.tw
886-3-571-2121

National Yunlin School of Science
    and Technology
Center for Small and Medium
    Business Innovation and Incubation
Yunlin
www.yuntech.edu.tw
886-5-534-2601 x 5155

Thailand

Bangkok University International
   College
Entrepreneurship Program
Bangkok
www.bu.ac.th
buic@bu.ac.th
66-2350-3635

United Arab Emirates

Dubai University
Entrepreneurship Training Program
Centre for Management and
   Professional Development
Dubai
www.duc.ac.ae
971-4-2072-603

United Kingdom

University of Aberdeen
Centre for Entrepreneurship
Business School
Aberdeen, Scotland
www.abdn.ac.uk/business/ce.shtml
44-122-427-2167

University of Abertay
PGDip Entrepreneurship
Dundee Business School
Dundee, Scotland
www.abertay.ac.uk
emquiries@abertay.ac.uk
44-138-230-8000

Aston University
Innovation Lab Europe
Aston Business School
Birmingham
www.abs.aston.ac.uk/newweb/
   research/ile
44-121-204-3000

University of Birmingham
The Entrepreneurship and
   Innovation Centre
Birmingham
www.res.bham.ac.uk/information/
   entrepreneurship
res-ent@bham.ac.uk
44-121-414-3898

Cambridge University
Centre for Entrepreneurial Learning
Cambridge
www.entrepreneurs.jims.cam.ac.uk
entrepreneurs@jims.cam.ac.uk
44-122-376-6900

Coventry University
Enterprise and Entrepreneurship
   Program
Coventry
www.coventry.ac.uk
44-247-688-7688

University of Derby
Centre for Entrepreneurial
   Management
The Derbyshire Business School
Derby
www.derby.ac.uk/cem
cem@derby.ac.uk
44-133-259-1896

University of Durham
Centre for Entrepreneurship
Durham Business School
Durham
www.dur.ac.uk/dbs/research/centre
44-191-334-5200

University of Brighton
Bright Ideas Program
Eastbourne Enterprise Hub
Brighton
www.brighton.ac.uk
44-127-360-0900

Glascow Caledonian University
Scottish Institute for Entrepreneurs
Glascow, Scotland
www.gcal.ac.uk
44-141-331-8784

University of Greenwich
Centre for Entrepreneurship
Business School
Greenwich, London
www.gre.ac.uk/schools/business/
   entrepreneur
44-208-331-9835

London Metropolitan University
Entrepreneurship Program
London
www.londonmet.ac.uk
44-207-423-0000

Kingston University
Small Business Research Centre
Faculty of Business
Surrey, London
www.kingston.ac.uk
44-116-207-8923

De Montfort University
Center for Research in Ethnic
   Minority Entrepreneurship
Leicester
www.creme-dmu.org.uk

University of Luton
Entrepreneurship and Business
    Management Program
School of Business
Luton
www.luton.ac.uk
44-158-274-3960

University of Newcastle
Enterprise Centre
Newcastle
www.ncl.ac.uk/teachingexcellence/
    teaching/enterprisecentre
44-115-846-6609

Nottingham Trent University
Business Innovation and Creation
    Team
School of Business
Nottingham
www.ntu.ac.uk/business_and_
    enterprise
44-115-941-8418

University of Paisley
Enterprise Studies Program
Business School
Paisley, Scotland
www.paisley.ac.uk/business
44-141-848-3000

University of Reading
Innovation & Entrepreneurship
    Program
Business School
Reading
www.rdg.ac.uk/business
44-118-378-8226

University of Manchester
Business Incubator
Manchester Business School
Manchester
www.mbs.ac.uk/services/incubator
incubator@mbs.ac.uk
44-161-275-6487

University of Nottingham
Institute for Enterprise and
    Innovation
Nottingham
www.nottingham.ac.uk
UNIEIEnquiries@nottingham.ac.uk
44-115-846-6609

Oxford University
Skoll Centre for Social
    Entrepreneurship
Said Business School
Oxford
www.sbs.ox.ac.uk
44-186-528-8838

University of Portsmouth
The Portsmouth Centre for
    Enterprise
Faculty of Technology
Portsmouth
www.port.ac.uk/departments/
    academic/enterprise
44-239-284-8484

The Robert Gordon University
Charles P. Skene Centre for
    Entrepreneurship
Aberdeen Business School
Aberdeen, Scotland
www.rgu.ac.uk/abs/centres
44-122-426-3895

University of Southhampton
Institute for Entrepreneurship
School of Management
Southhampton
www.ife.soton.ac.uk
44-238-059-8899

University of Strathcylde
Hunter Centre for Entrepreneurship
Glascow, Scotland
www.entrepreneur.strath.ac.uk
44-141-548-3482

University of Ulster
School of Marketing,
    Entrepreneurship and Strategy
Belfast and Londonderry, No. Ireland
www.ulst.ac.uk
business@ulster.ac.uk
44-289-036-6351

University of Stirling
Centre for Entrepreneurship
Stirling, Scotland
www.entrepreneurship.stir.ac.uk
44-178-647-3171

University of Teeside
Centre for Entrepreneurship and
    SME Development
Teeside Business School
Middlesbrough
www.tees.ac.uk
44-164-234-2807

University of Warwick
Centre for Small and Medium Sized
    Enterprises
Warwick Business School
Coventry
http://users.wbs.ac.uk/group/csme
44-247-652-3747

SELECTED WEB SITES

National Government

Australian Department of Small Business	www.smallbusiness.gov.au
Canadian Rural Information Services	www.rural.gc.ca
Central Contractor Registration	www.ccr.gov
Federal Government Official Web Portal	www.firstgov.gov
FedWorld (helpful guide)	www.fedworld.gov
HK Small Medium Information Centre	www.sme.gcn.gov.hk
Industry Canada	www.strategis.ic.gc.ca
Internal Revenue Service	www.irs.gov
IRS Employer Identification Number	www.irs.gov/businesses/small
Minority Business Development Agency	www.mbda.gov
National Women's Business Council	www.nwbc.gov
New Zealand Trade and Enterprise	www.nzte.govt.nz
U.S. Small Business Administration	www.sba.gov
SBA Library	www.sba.gov/library
SBA Office of Advocacy, Statistics and Research	www.sba.gov/advo/research
Small Business Services	www.sbs.gov.uk
SCORE (Service Corps of Retired Executives)	www.score.org
Statistics USA	www.stat-usa.gov
U.S. Business Advisor	www.business.gov
U.S. Census Bureau	www.census.gov
U.S. Copyright Office	www.copyright.gov
U.S. Department of Labor	www.dol.gov
U.S. General Services Administration	www.gsa.gov

U.S. Patent and Trademark Office	www.uspto.gov
U.S. Treasury	www.irs.ustreas.gov

National Organizations

General Information

American Franchisee Association	www.franchisee.org
The American Small Business Association	www.asba.org
Association for Enterprise Opportunity	www.microenterpriseworks.org
Association for Small Business Development Centers	www.asbdc-us.org
Association of Marketing Students	www.deca.org
Biotechnology Young Entrepreneurs Scheme	www.biotechnologyyes.co.uk
Business Information Provider	www.edgar-online.com
The Business of Technology	www.redherring.com
Canada Business Service Centres	www.cbsc.org
Center for Rural Entrepreneurship	www.ruraleship.org
Coleman Foundation	www.colemanfoundation.org
Draper Fisher Jurvetson Entrepreneurship Resources	www.drapervc.com
Edward Lowe Foundation	www.lowe.org
Entrepreneur Action	www.entrepreneuraction.co.uk
Entrepreneurship Institute of Canada	www.entinst.ca
eWeb @ St. Louis University	http://eweb.slu.edu
The Franchise Handbook Online	www.franchise1.com
Foundation of Small Business	www.fsb.org.uk
The Family Business Network	www.fb_-i.org
Family Firm Institute	www.ffi.org
FRANCORP	www.francorp.com
Future Business Leaders of America	www.fbla.pbl.org
Garage Technology Ventures	www.garage.com
Genus, Consultants to Family Business	www.genusresources.com
Global Information Net for SMEs	www.gin.sme.ne.jp
Hewlett Packard Small Business Center	www.hp.com

Idea Café	www.businessownersideacafe.com
The Incubator—Technology Innovation Center	www.theincubator.com
The Indus Entrepreneurs	www.tie.org
Industrial Development Corporation of South Africa	www.idc.co.za
Industry Reports	www.valuationresources.com
International Franchise Association	www.franchise.org
International Small Business Consortium	www.isbc.com
Junior Achievement	www.ja.org
U.S. Jaycees International	www.usjaycees.org
Kauffman Foundation	www.kauffman.org
Kauffman Foundation Entreworld	www.entreworld.com
Making It!	www.makingittv.com
MassMutual Family Business Network	www.massmutual.com
Microsoft Small Business Center	www.microsoft.com/smallbusiness
Lippincott Library of Entrepreneurship and Small Business Resources	www.fastcompany.com
National Association for the Self-Employed	www.nase.org
National Association of Home Based Business	www.usahomebusiness.com
National Collegiate Inventors and Innovators Alliance	www.nciia.org
National Business Incubation Association	www.nbia.org
National Small Business Association	www.nsba.biz
Netpreneur Exchange of the Morino Institute	http://netpreneur.org
New Zealand Entrepreneurs Club	www.entrepreneur.ac.nz
Nussbaum Center for Entrepreneurship	http://nussbaum.com
OECD Initiative on Small and Medium Enterprises	www.oecd.org
Pilot Action for Startups: Europe	www.cordis.lu/paxis
Rise Business	www.riseb.org
SAGE (Students for the Advancement of Global Entrepreneurship	www.csuchico.edu/sage

SIFE (Students in Free Enterprise)	www.sife.org
The Small Business Advancement Center	www.sbaer.uca.edu
Small Business Advisor	www.isquare.com
Small Business Benefit Association	www.sbba.com
Small Business Gateway	www.bgateway.com
Small Business Solutions	http://smallbusiness.dnb.com
Small and Home-Based Business Resources	www.bizoffice.com
Small and Home-Based Business Library	www.bizoffice.com/library
SME Information of Japan	www.sme.ne.jp/japane.html
Startups	www.startups.co.uk
Swiss Small Enterprise Development	www.intercoop.ch/sed/main
Umsobomvu Youth Fund South Africa	www.uyf.org.za
U.S. Association for Small Business and Entrepreneurship	www.usasbe.org
U.S. Chamber of Commerce	www.uschamber.com
Young Entrepreneurs Organization	www.yeo.org

Minority Entrepreneurs

Asian American Alliance	www.asianamericanalliance.com
Asian American Economic Development and Entrepreneurship	www.aaedc.org
Asian-Pacific Management Forum	www.apmforum.com
Asian Women in Business	www.awib.org
Black Enterprise	www.blackenterprise.com
Hispanic Business	www.hispanicbusiness.com
Hispanic Net	www.hispanic-net.org
Latin-American Business Link	www.labl.com
National Minority Business Council	www.nmbc.org
National Minority Supplier Development Council	www.nmsdcus.org

Women Entrepreneurs

Alliance of Women Entrepreneurs	www.awe-westmichigan.org
American Woman's Economic Development Corp	www.awed.org

Catalyst Women	www.catalystswomen.org
eWomen Network	www.ewomennetwork.com
Forum for Women Entrepreneurs	www.fwe.org
Moms Network Exchange for Home-Based Businesses	www.momsnetwork.com
National Association of Woman Business Owners	www.nawbo.org
National Foundation of Women Business Owners	www.nfwbo.org
National Women Business Owners Corporation	www.nwboc.org
WIN—Connecting Women and Capital	www.winwomen.org
Women in Technology International	www.wti.com
Women's Business Development Center	www.wbdc.org
Women's Chamber of Commerce	www.uswomenschamber.com
Women's Opportunity Resources Center	www.worc-pa.com
Women's Work	http://wwork.com

Finance

Angel Capital Network	http://activecapital.org
Angel Deals	www.venturepreneurs.com
Blue Tree Allied Angels	www.bluetreealliedangels.com
Capital Network Securities	www.thecapitalnetwork.com
Community of Independent Accountants	www.accountantsworld.com
CPA Finder	www.cpafinder.com
Directory of Venture Capital Firms and Tradeshows	www.vfinance.com
Early-Stage Venture Capital Firm	www.prologventures.com
Garage Technology Ventures	www.garage.com
GE Small Business Finance	www.ge.com/capital/smallbiz
Growthink Capital Funding Research	www.growthinkresearch.com
Lore Associates	www.loreassociates.com
Money Hunt	www.moneyhunter.com
National Association of Small Business Accountants	www.smallbizaccountants.com
National Venture Capital Association	www.nvca.org

Operation Hope Loan Center	www.operationhope.org
PricewaterhouseCoopers Money Tree VC Survey	www.pwcmoneytree.com
Private Equity Network	www.privateequity.com
RiverVest Venture Partners	www.rivervest.com
The Tax Prophet	www.taxprophet.com
Venture Capital Information	www.vcfodder.com
Venture One Research	www.ventureone.com
Yahoo! Finance	http://finance.yahoo.com

Law

Business Law Lounge	www.lectlaw.com
Delaware Incorporation	www.incorporate.com
Find a Lawyer	www.findlaw.com
Get a Patent Online	www.internet-patents.com
Incorporating Your Business	www.bizfilings.com
Internet Legal Research Group	www.ilrg.com
Lawyers.com	www.lawyers.com
NOLO Law for All	www.nolo.com

Planning

Biz Plan It	www.bizplanit.com
Business Plan Software	www.planware.org
Center for Business Planning	www.businessplans.org
Growthink Business Plan Consulting	www.growthink.com
More Business	www.MoreBusiness.com
Sample Business Plans	www.bplans.com
SBA Business Plan Basics	www.sba.gov
WSJ Center for Entrepreneurs	http://wsj.mininplan.com

Marketing

Advance Emarketing	www.advancedemarketing.com
Cliff Allen on Marketing	www.allen.com
E-commerce News	www.internet.com
Electronic Commerce	www.ecommerce-guide.com

Guerilla Marketing	www.gmarketing.com
Impact Business Developers	www.impactbizdev.com
Internet Marketing Center	www.marketingtips.com
Sell It on the Web	www.sellitontheweb.com
Solutions for Marketers	www.clickz.com
Understanding USA	www.understandingusa.com
Web Marketing Today	www.wilsonweb.com
Zap Data Industry Reports	www.zapdata.com

Insurance

Insurance Comparison Shopping	www.insweb.com
Insurance Industry Network	www.iiin.com
Insurance Shopping	www.insure.com
Insurance Services Network	www.isn-inc.com

Local Organizations (Examples)

Atlantic Canada Opportunities Agency	www.acoa.ca
Center for Women and Enterprise, Boston	www.cweboston.org
Chicago—Back of the Yards	www.bync.org
Chicagoland Chamber of Commerce	www.chicagolandchamber.org
The Chicagoland Entrepreneurial Center	www.chicagolandec.org
Colorado Women's Chamber of Commerce	www.cwcc.org
Entrepreneurs' Forum of Greater Philadelphia	www.efgp.org
Florida Angel Investors	www.floridaangel.com
Florida Venture Forum	www.flvencap.org
Illinois Small Business Development Association	www.isbda.org
L.A. Regional Technology Alliance	www.larta.org
Minnesota Technology, Inc	www.minnesotatechnology.org
MIT Enterprise Forum	www.mitforumcambridge.org
Nebraska Development Network	www.nol.org
Ontario Business Service Centre	www.cbsc.org/ontario

Pittsburgh Regional Alliance	www.pittsburghregion.org
San Gabriel Valley Economic Partnership	www.valleyconnect.com
Smaller Business Association of New England	www.sbane.org
Southern California Minority Business Development Council	www.scmbdc.org
Sydney Business Enterprise Centre	www.sydneybec.com.au
Tie-Pittsburgh	www.tiepgh.org
Utah Angels	www.utahangels.org
Welsh Development Agency	www.wda.co.uk
Western Economic Diversification Canada	www.wd.gc.ca

Online Publications (Examples)

Advertising Age	www.adage.com
Asia Inc. Online	www.asia-inc.com
Asian Wall Street Journal Online	http://online.wsj.com/public/asia
BBC	www.bbc.co.uk
BizWoman	www.bizjournals.com
Black Enterprise Magazine	www.blackenterprise.com
Bloomberg Online	www.bloomberg.com
Boulder City Business Report	www.bcbr.com
Business Day, Johannesburg	www.businessday.co.za
Business Week	www.businessweek.com
Canadian Broadcasting Corp.	www.cbc.com
Crains Chicago Business	www.crainschicagobusiness.com
Crains New York	www.crainsny.com
Daily Journal of Commerce (Portland, OR)	www.djc-or.com
Dow Jones	www.dowjones.com
EU Affairs	www.euaffairs.com
Various Local Business Journals	www.bizjournals.com
Direct Marketers News	www.dmnews.com
The Economist	www.economist.com
Entrepreneur	www.entrepreneur.com

Family Business Magazine	www.familybusinessmagazine.com
Financial Post nationalpost/financialpost	www.canada.com/national/
Financial Times	www.ft.com
Forbes	www.forbes.com
Fortune	www.fortune.com
Home Business Journal	www.homebizjour.com
Inc.	www.inc.com
International Herald Tribune	www.iht.com
The Japan Times	Online www.japantimes.co.jp
Journal of New England Technology	www.masshightech.com
L.A. Times Small Business	www.latimes.com/business
Minority Business Entrepreneur	www.mbemag.com
National Business Review, Auckland	www.nbr.co.nz
New York Times	www.nytimes.com/specials/
Northern Colorado Business Report	www.ncbr.com
Orange County Business Journal	www.ocbj.com
San Diego Business Journal	www.signonsandiego.com
Seattle Daily Journal of Commerce	www.djc.com
Sydney Morning Herald	www.smh.com.au
The (Singapore) Straits Times Online	http://straitstimes.asia1.com.sg
The Times of London	www.timesonline.co.uk
The Times of India http://timesofindia.indiatimes.com	
USA Today business/front.htm	www.usatoday.com/money/small-
Wall Street Journal Center for Entrepreneurs	www.startupjournal.com
Wyoming Business Report	www.wyomingbusinessreport.com

SELECTED BOOKS

Textbooks and How-To Books

Building a Dream: A Canadian Guide to Starting Your Own Business, Walter S. Good

The Complete Canadian Small Business Guidebook, Douglas Gray and Diana Gray

The Entrepreneurial Mindset, by Rita Gunther McGrath and Ian MacMillan

Entrepreneurship: A Process Perspective, by Rovert A. Brown and Scott S. Shane

Entrepreneurship for Dummies, by Kathleen Allen

Entrepreneurship: Strategies and Resources, by Marc Dollinger

Entrepreneurship: Theory, Process and Practice, by Donald P. Kuratko and Richard M. Hodgetts

Entrepreneur's Toolkit: Tools and Techniques to Launch and Grow Your New Business, HBR Essentials Series

Essentials of Entrepreneurship and Small Business Management, by Thomas Zimmer

Home-Based Businesses for Dummies, by Paul and Sarah Edwards

Home Networking for Dummies, by Kathy Ivens

How to Franchise Your Own Business, by G. Nieman and J. Barber

The New Venture Handbook: Everything You Need to Know to Start and Run Your Own Business, by Ronald E. Merrill and Henry D. Sedgewick

New Venture Mechanics, by Karl H. Vesper

The Portable MBA in Entrepreneurship, William Bygrave (editor)

Restaurant Management: A Comprehensive Guide to Successfully Owning and Running a Restaurant, by John James and Dan Baldwin

Small Business Kit for Dummies, Richard D. Harroch

Small Business Kit, by Joanna Krotz, Ben Ryan, and John Pierce

Specialty Shop Retailing: How to Run Your Own Store, by Carol L. Schroeder

Start Your Own Business, by Rieva Lesonsky

The Ultimate Small Business Guide, Ultimate Business Guide Series

Biographies, Histories, and Case Studies

Blue Mountain: Turning Dreams into Reality, by Susan Polis Schutz

The Difference Between God and Larry Ellison: Inside Oracle Corporation, by Mike Wilson

Direct from DELL, by M. Dell and C. Friedman

Entrepreneurs in History: Success vs. Failure Entrepreneurial Role Models, by Emerson Klees

Harvests of Joy, by Robert Mondavi

Losing My Virginity, by Richard Branson

Made in Japan, by A. Morita, E. Reinsgold and M. Shimomura

McDonald's: Behind the Arches, by John F. Love

Only the Paranoid Survive, by Andy Grove

Sam Walton: Made in America, by Sam Walton

Success Stories: How Eleven of Japan's Most Interesting Businesses Came to Be, by Leonard Koren

We Were Burning: Japanese Entrepreneurs and the Forging of the Electronic Age, by Bob Johnstone

E-business

Burn Rate: How I Survived the Gold Rush Years on the Internet, by Michael Wolff

Competing on Internet Time: Lessons from Netscape and Its Battle with Microsoft, by Michael Cusumano

eBay Business, by Joseph T. Sinclair

E Myth Mastery, by Michael Gerber

The E Myth Revisited, by Michael Gerber

Entrepreneurship.Com, by Tim Burns

Start Your Own Business on eBay, by Jacquelyn Lynn

Unleashing the Power of eBay, by Dennis Prince

Finance

Attracting Equity Investors, by Dean A. Shepherd and Evan J. Douglas

Budgeting for a Small Business, by Terry Dickey

Canadian Business Financing Handbook, Gary A. Fitchett

Extending Credit and Collecting Cash, by Lynn Harrison

Financial and Cost Analysis for Engineering and Technology Management, by Hank Riggs

Financing the Small Business, by Charles H. Green

How to Raise Capital: Techniques and Strategies for Financing and Valuing Your Small Business, by Jeffry Timmons, Stephen Spinelli, and Andrew Zacharakis

Idiot's Guide to Buying and Selling a Business, by Ed Paulson

Keeping the Books: Basic Recordkeeping and Accounting for the Successful Small Business, by Linda Pinson

Raising Money: Venture Funding and How to Get It, by Ronald E. Merrill

SBA Loans: A Step-by-step Guide, by Patrick D. O'Hara

Tax Savvy for Small Business, by Frederick W. Daily

Tax Smarts for Small Business, by James O. Parker
Venture Capital, Entrepreneurship and Public Policy, Vesa Kannianen (editor)

Franchising

Franchise Bible, by Erwin J. Keup
Franchising Dreams, by Peter M. Birkeland
Franchising: Pathway to Wealth Creation, by Stephen Spinelli and others

General Books

The Art of the Steal: How to Protect Yourself and Your Business, by Frank W. Abagnale
The Best Home Businesses for People 50+, by Paul and Sarah Edwards
Built to Last, by Jim Collins and Jerry Porras
Entrepreneurship in Action, by Mary Coulter
Entrepreneurship in the Hospitality, Tourism and Leisure Industries, by Alison Morrison
Geeks and Geezers, by Warren Bennis and Robert J. Thomas
Harvard Business Review on Entrepreneurship, by Amar Bhldt and others
Negotiate This, by Herb Cohen
New Business Ventures and the Entrepreneur, by Howard Stevenson and others
New Venture Creation: Entrepreneurship for the 21ˢᵗ Century, by Jeffry Timmons and Stephen Spinelli
The One-to-One Future, by Don Peppers and others
Regional Advantage, by A. Saxenian
Startup, by Jerry Kaplan
The Start-up Entrepreneur, by James R. Cook
We've Got Fired, by Harvey McKay
What I Learned from Wal-Mart, by Michael Bersdall
Zen Entrepreneurship: Walking the Path of the Career Warrior, by Rizwan Virk

Global Entrepreneurship

Entrepreneurial Research: Global Perspectives, by Sue Birley and Ian MacMillan
Entrepreneurship in a Global Context, by Sue Birley and Ian MacMillan
Entrepreneurship in Asia Pacific: Past, Present Future, by Leo Paul Dana
International Entrepreneurship, by Sue Birley and Ian MacMillan

Innovation

Corporate Venturing: Creating New Businesses within the Firm, by Zena Block and Ian MacMillan
Innovation and Entrepreneurship, by Peter F. Drucker
Old Dogs, New Tricks, by Warren Bennis

Organizing Genius: The Secrets of Creative Collaboration, by Warren Bennis and
Patricia Ward Biederman

Law

Business Law, by Robert W. Emerson
The Entrepreneur's Guide to Business Law, by Constance Bagley and Craig E. Dauchy
The Legal Guide for Small Business, by Charles P. Lickson

Marketing

Crossing the Chasm, by Geoff Moore
Customer Inspired Quality, by James G. Shaw
Customer Mania, by Ken Blanchard
Discover Your Product's Hidden Potential, by Ian MacMillan
Guerilla Marketing, by Jay Conrad Levinson
How to Drive the Competition Crazy, by Guy Kawasaki
Idiots Guide to Marketing, by Sarah White
Inside the Tornado, by Geoff Moore
The Little Red Book of Selling, by Jeffrey Gitomer
Marketing and Entrepreneurship, Gerald E. Hills (editor)
Marketing for Dummies, by Alexander Hiam
On Target, by Laura Rowley
Real Time Marketing, by Regis McKenna
Relationship Marketing: Successful Strategies for the Age of the Customer, by Regis
McKenna

Planning

Business Plans for Dummies, by Paul Tiffany and Steven D. Peterson
Business Plans Made Easy, by Mark Henricks and John Riddle
Business Plans That Work, by Alice H. Magus and Steve Crow
The Complete Book of Business Plans, by Joseph A. Covello and Brian J. Hazelgren
Fashion Entrepreneurship: Retail Business Planning, by Michele Granger and
Tina Sterling
The Ernst and Young Business Plan Guide, by Eric Siegel, Brian R. Ford, and Jay
M. Burnstein
The Successful Business Plan: Secrets and Strategies, by Rhonda Abrams

Social Issues

Jesus, Entrepreneur, by Laurie Beth Jones
Small Business Entrepreneurship: An Ethics and Human Relations Perspective, by
Lavern S. Urlacher

Social Entrepreneurship: The Art of Mission-Based Venture Development, by Peter C. Brinckerhoft

Technology

Engineering Your Start-up: A Guide for the Hi-Tech Entrepreneur, by Michael L. Baird

High Tech StartUp, by John L. Nesheim

High-Tech Ventures: The Guide for Entrepreneurial Success, by C. Gordon Bell, with John E. McNamara

Marketing High Technology: An Insider's View, by Regis Mckenna

The Silicon Valley Edge, by Chong-Moon Lee and others

Women and Minorities

About My Sister's Business: The Black Women's Road Map to Successful Entrepreneursip, by Fran Harris and Terrie Williams

Black Entrepreneurship in America, by Shelley Green

Confronting the Odds: African American Entrepreneurship in Cleveland, by Bessie House-Soremekun

The Girls' Guide to Starting Your Own Business, by Caitlin Friedman and Kimberly Yorio

If You've Raised the Kids, You Can Manage Anything, by Ann Crittenden

References

Adams, P. E. *Fail-Proof Your Business: Beat the Odds and Be Successful*. Los Angeles, CA: Adams-Hall Publishing, 1999.

Aronoff, C., and Ward, J. L. *Contemporary Entrepreneurs: Profiles of Entrepreneurs and the Businesses They Started*. Detroit, Mich.: Omnigraphics, Inc., 1992.

Block, Z., and MacMillan, I. C. *Corporate Venturing: Creating New Businesses within the Firm*. Boston, Mass.: Harvard Business School Press, 1993.

Branson, R. *Losing My Virginity*. New York: Random House, 1998.

Brechner, B. "A Question of Judgment," *Flying*, May 1981, 47–52.

Bygrave, W. D. *The Portable MBA in Entrepreneurship*. New York: Wiley, 1998.

"Clarett Blocked from Draft." *The Daily Yomiuri*, Apr. 12, 2004, pp. 8.

Dell, M. *Direct from DELL*. New York: HarperCollins, 1999.

Fadiman, C. (ed.). *Bartlett's Book of Anecdotes*. New York: Little, Brown, 1985.

Gates, B. *The Road Ahead*. New York: Viking Penguin, 1995.

The Global Entrepreneurship Monitor (GEM Report). Boston: Babson College and the London Business School, 2004.

Grove, A. *Only the Paranoid Survive*. New York: Currency, 1996.

Habib, D. G. "A Model of Efficiency." *Sports Illustrated* via *The Daily Yomiuri*. Tokyo: Apr. 26, 2004, p. 22.

Hatamura, Y. *Learning from Failure*. Tokyo: World Association Publishing, 2002.

Hilton, C. *Be My Guest*. Englewood Cliffs, N.J.: Prentice Hall, 1957.

Hopkins, J. "Italian Ice Entrepreneurs Fear Getting Frozen Out of Shelf Space." *USA Today*, Aug. 20, 2004, pp. B1–B2.

Horowitz, A. *The Dumbest Moments in Business History*. New York: Penguin, 2004.

Horwitt, D. "This Hard-Earned Money Comes Stuffed in Their Genes." *The Washington Post* via *The Daily Yomiuri*. Tokyo: Apr. 21, 2004, p. 21.

Johnstone, R. *We Were Burning: Japanese Entrepreneurs and the Forging of the Electronic Age*. New York: Basic Books, 1999.

Kepner, T. "A-Rod Embraces Learning Curve." *International Herald Tribune*, Apr. 5, 2004, p. 14.

Klees, E. *Entrepreneurs in History: Success vs. Failure Entrepreneurial Role Models*. Rochester, N.Y.: Cameo Press, 1995.

Koren, L. *Success Stories: How Eleven of Japan's Most Interesting Businesses Came to Be*. San Francisco: Chronicle Books, 1990.

Koseki, M. "Maverick Metal Molder Happy Solving Big Boy's Problems." *The Japan Times*, May 19, 2002, p. 8.

Kuemmerle, W. "A Test for the Fainthearted." *Harvard Business Review*. Boston, Mass.: Harvard Business School, 2002, pp. 122–127.

Love, J. F. *McDonald's: Behind the Arches*. New York: Bantam Books, 1995.

Mair, G. *Oprah Winfrey: The Real Story*. New York: Carol Publishing Group, 1994.

Miller, K. "Your Spaceship Awaits." *Life*, Oct. 22, 2004, pp. 6–10.

Mintzberg, H., Lampel, J. Q., Quin, J. B., and Ghoshal, S. *The Strategy Process*. Englewood Cliffs, N.J.: Prentice Hall, 2002.

Mondavi, R. *Harvests of Joy*. Orlando: Harcourt Brace, 1998.

Morita, A., Reinsgold, E., and Shimomura, M. *Made in Japan*. New York: E. P. Dutton, 1986.

Okeson, B., and Wakao, A. "Wal-Mart's Japanese Makeover." *International Herald Tribune*, July 16, 2004, p. B4.

Otake, T. "Trying to Learn From Failure Suddenly All the Rage." *The Japan Times*, Sept. 18, 2002, p. 5.

Panati, C. *Extraordinary Origins of Everyday Things*. New York: Harper & Row, 1987.

Poundstone, W. *Biggest Secrets: More Uncensored Truth About All Sorts of Stuff You are Never Supposed to Know*. New York: Morrow , 1993.

"PowerBar's Cocreater Maxwell Dead at Age 51." Reuters. *The Japan Times*, Mar. 23, 2004, p. 6.

"Red, White and Brew." *Metropolis*. Tokyo, Sept. 3, 2004, p. 17.Richtel, M. "End is Swift and Sudden For an Internet Company." *The New York Times*. Nov. 6, 2000, pp. C5.

Schlender, B. "Why Andy Grove Can't Sleep." *Fortune*, July 10, 1995, p. 92.

Sorkin, A. R. "From Big Idea to Big Bust: The Wild Ride of Boo.com." *The New York Times*, Dec. 13, 2000, p. H3.

Spinelli, S., with Timmons, J. *New Venture Creation for the 21st Century*. New York: McGraw-Hill, 2003.

Taylor, C. "Seek and You Shall Find." *Time*, Apr. 26, 2004.

Uranaka, T. "Founder of Don Quijote Empire Revels in Breaking All the Rules." *The Japan Times*, Jan. 1, 2004, p. 6.

Walton, S. *Sam Walton: Made in America*. New York: Bantam Books, 1993.

Wawro, T. *Radicals & Visionaries*. Irvine, Calif.: Entrepreneur Press, 2000.

Wilson, M. *The Difference Between God and Larry Ellison: Inside Oracle Corporation*. New York: William Morrow and Company, 1997.

www.aqa.issuebits.com
www.benjerry.com/our_company/our_history/timeline/index.cfm
www.ko-cosmos.co.jp
www.orfaleafamily.org/profile.htm
www.tjcinnamons.com./tj01.html
www.ur.wmich.edu/magazine

Index